The Process of Politics

About the Author

Jorgen Rasmussen, at present Associate Professor of Political Science at Vanderbilt University, was formerly Assistant Professor of Political Science at the University of Arizona in Tucson, and in 1968–1969 was Visiting Associate Professor of Government at Columbia University. He received both his M.A. and Ph.D. (1962) in political science from the University of Wisconsin and was selected a Woodrow Wilson Fellow, a Danforth Fellow, and a Social Science Research Council Research Training Fellow in Britain. Author of *Retrenchment and Revival: A Study of the Contemporary British Liberal Party* and *The Relations of the Profumo Rebels with Their Local Parties*, Professor Rasmussen has also contributed to numerous scholarly journals in the United States and abroad and has served as a review consultant for *Choice*.

THE PROCESS

OF POLITICS

A Comparative Approach

Jorgen Rasmussen, Vanderbilt University

ATHERTON PRESS, INC. NEW YORK 1969

Address all inquiries to:
Atherton Press, Inc.
70 Fifth Avenue
New York 10011

Library of Congress Catalog Card Number 78-80903
FIRST EDITION

Manufactured in the United States of America
Designed by Paula Wiener

Preface

In writing this book I have tried to produce a text suitable for
introductory courses in comparative politics regardless of whether
the instructor uses the vertical, country-by-country approach or
the horizontal, functional approach. Students in courses that
focus on several foreign governments could use this text as an
introduction to the study of comparative politics, and then consider whatever countries the instructor prefers. A study of each
country's political system could include an investigation of the
extent to which the general findings presented here hold true in
any particular political system. This procedure would help students identify the special circumstances in a given country which
produce a measure of uniqueness in its political system. Knowledge of both a country's political uniqueness and its ordinariness
should enhance students' understanding of that country's political process and structure. Proceeding this way also can help to
make the country-by-country approach more comparative and
analytical, rather than simply a study of foreign governments.

The instructor who prefers the functional approach could
make this book the core around which to organize the course.
He could assign supplementary readings on topics or functions

he wishes to pursue in greater detail. Because this text provides both an introduction to the field and the framework for further study, it would help to clarify for students the interrelation of the various functions presented in the additional reading assignments.

Another possible use of this text is as a part of the first course in political science. In this case, the book would help students gain a knowledge of basic concerns and procedures of the discipline of political science within the field of comparative politics. The discussion in this book of the most significant findings about various key political functions would also introduce students to some of the basic facts of the discipline.

An introductory book should not be bogged down with detailed footnotes. On the other hand, those whose work has advanced our knowledge should be credited, and students should be introduced to those thinkers and their writings as well as to their ideas. I have tried to satisfy both aims through summary footnotes which indicate for each chapter the research on which it is based.

Because I did not wish to write a volume the size of a dictionary, and because I wanted this work to be a truly comparative synthesis, I originally intended to use as sources only those studies which focused on more than one country or were clearly replicative. Although I adhered to this plan as much as possible, the paucity of studies which could qualify as sources proved much greater than anticipated. Thus, I have been forced at times to rely on single-country studies. The deplorable lack of empirical, comparative studies was a constant frustration and the major obstacle to completing this introductory summary.

Because authors' appreciative comments are of no interest to the reader, I will confine my thanks to Charles McCall, who took time from a busy schedule to read virtually all the manuscript for this book and to comment on it. I am very grateful for his assistance.

JORGEN RASMUSSEN

Contents

Preface   vii

1. The Significance and Aims of Comparative Politics   1

     Why Bother to Study Politics?   1
     Comparative Studies' Value for Political Theory   4
     An Approach to Political Analysis   8

2. Environment, Culture, and Politics   21

     Requisites of Independence and Democracy   21
     Political Culture's Contribution to Democracy   32
     Social Factors Nurturing Self-confident Citizens   40

3. Varieties of Political Change   47

     Obstacles to Evolutionary Studies   47
     Political and Economic Development in Indus-
         trially Advanced Nations   50
     The Impact of Development in New Nations   68
     Extraconstitutional Change   74

4. Expressing and Focusing Demands
     for Authoritative Decisions   83

     Class and Political Activity   84
     Parties, the Party System, and the Political System   91
     Political Participation through Interest Groups   102

5. Policy-making and Implementing Structures 115

The Contrast between Institutions and Structures 115
The Chimera of Constitutional Tinkering 118
Parliamentary Structures' Influence on Parties 128
The Misleading Federal-Unitary Dichotomy 137
Varieties of Bureaucratic Structures 142

6. Who Governs? 153

Characteristics of Political Leaders 154
Does an Elite Rule? 162

7. Research Goals for Comparative Politics 179

Notes 195
For Further Reading 207
Index 217

The Process of Politics

Chapter 1

The Significance and Aims
of Comparative Politics

Why Bother to Study Politics?

If all men were hermits, anarchy would be a sensible form of political organization. The man who seeks to live in isolation, to make himself an island, denies a portion of his humanity. "He who is unable to live in society, or who has no need because he is sufficient for himself," Aristotle observed centuries ago, "must be either a beast or a god."

Most men prefer a more gregarious life. They associate with others to gain companionship and to satisfy their wants and needs more efficiently. By assigning particular tasks to individuals who have developed relevant skills and by working in groups, men are able to accomplish what they could not do, or could not do as well, by themselves.

Once men begin to deal with each other, once they begin to become a group, an association, a society, they cannot be left unguided or unregulated to follow their individual values and goals. To assume that some invisible hand will order their relations rationally to the greatest benefit of all is a utopian dream. That everyone but one man wishes to use a river for swimming and fishing matters little, if the one dissenter owns the slaughter-house that empties its offal into the river. Unless such conflicts of interest are to be settled by violence, recognized channels and procedures for arbitrating them—political structures—must be established. The purpose of such structures is not to eliminate conflict—they are neither productive of nor needed in a millennial society, religious or Marxian, in which men live in perfect harmony and contentment—but rather to keep conflict within acceptable bounds so that men can live together peaceably and can form a society, despite their differences.

A society without political institutions can hardly be called a society; it is merely an aggregate. It does not resemble the nineteenth-century romantics' pristine idyl of the life of the "noble savage," but corresponds instead to the "state of nature" described by the seventeenth-century political philosopher Thomas Hobbes as "that condition called Warre; and such a warre, as is of every man, against every man—[a life] solitary, poor, nasty, brutish, and short." Not surprisingly, anthropologists have discovered that primitive societies empower their leaders to make rules binding upon all their members. Even these societies have political institutions. "Man," asserted Aristotle, "is by nature a political animal"; man is necessarily involved in politics, even if only as a passive subject. Politics—the process of governing—coextends with human life.

However, this characteristic does not distinguish politics from morality, religion, or family relations, to cite only a few examples. Nor is politics distinctive in involving authority and power. Many individuals and groups wield authority, even power, over others—such as parents over their children and churches over their members. Politics is unique in being the only process through which authoritative decisions are made which are applicable to an entire society and legitimately enforceable by sanctions.

Unfortunately, the effects of this process are contradictory. Although politics enables men to settle their conflicts more maturely, in a more civilized way, it also permits them to gain their way by coercing others even more effectively than they could if such a process did not exist. To control government is to possess the power to reward and penalize significantly—to tax incomes exceeding $10,000 at 50 percent, to award multimillion-dollar defense contracts to one business rather than to another, to provide educational benefits to war veterans. To control government is to be able to employ authoritative sanctions to assist imposing one set of values upon everyone—to fine those in Boston who sell banned books, to penalize those in Connecticut who circulate birth control information, to jail those in South Africa who oppose apartheid. To control government is to be empowered to kill thousands, even millions. Although the Jewish genocide in Nazi Germany may have failed to illustrate this power personally to most Americans, the 1962 Cuban missile crisis gave us an ample demonstration of it.

In *The English Constitution*, Walter Bagehot, a nineteenth-century student of British politics, wrote of Queen Victoria and the Prince of Wales: "It is nice to trace how the actions of a retired widow and an unemployed youth became of such importance." To adapt that comment to October 1962, it is fascinating to investigate how the actions of an elderly former blacksmith and an unemployed young man could determine whether millions of people should die or suffer excruciatingly. Governmental power undoubtedly affects everyone; control of such power can hardly be a matter of indifference.

Politics, then, is pervasive and momentous. However, its study is justifiable not only because it examines such extensive power and seeks to discover who gets what, and how, but because politics offers man innumerable opportunities to develop his most essential characteristic—the ability to solve problems rationally—and thus to become more fully human.

These opportunities are especially valuable for stimulating human growth when encountered in a political context, for in politics man confronts concrete conflicts, not abstract conundrums divorced from reality. The sharply distinct blacks and whites which characterize abstract problems blend into shades of gray when man must choose among real alternatives. You may strongly support free speech, but do you believe a high school teacher should be allowed to lecture his class that the United States government is so dominated by capitalist warmongers that it should be overthrown? Should a court limit news reports of trials of heinous crimes to help insure that hostile public opinion does not bias the jurors, or does this restriction of news violate freedom of the press? Justice is much more difficult to distinguish in the concrete than the abstract. Furthermore, concrete decisions have real, not merely speculative, effects. The politician's choice, unlike the philosopher's, matters, and he never can eradicate his mistakes completely. He cannot return the pieces to their original position and move pawn to queen four rather than to king four.

A process which, through binding rules, rewards, and penalties, directs men's lives to their benefit or detriment, a process which man cannot escape without ceasing to be a man, and a process which offers man wide scope to develop the rationality and ethical sensitivity that distinguish him from other animals is a process which deserves study. This study is, indeed, an indispensable response to the classical Greek injunction, "Know thyself." He who ignores this study merits the word the Greeks applied to those who took no part in public affairs—idiot.

Comparative Studies' Value for Political Theory

But why study foreign political systems? Wouldn't it be more worthwhile to improve your understanding of your own nation's political system rather than to divert your attention to governments that you cannot influence and that affect you only indirectly and perhaps marginally? Who, other than those residing there, cares how the government of Sierra Leone operates? These questions are best answered by considering what political scientists hope to accomplish.

Political scientists seek to substantiate, empirically, theories of politics that interrelate political functions, structures, and behavior with each other and with their environment. Such verified theories would not only help to satisfy the desire to understand more fully who controls government's awesome power for what purposes, but would also aid in anticipating the probable effects of various policies and decisions. Guided by such knowledge, political scientists could evaluate projected political action more expertly and thus offer more valuable counsel. Also, they could more wisely propose structural and procedural reforms for particular political systems which would enable those systems to fulfill their functions more beneficially.

To construct these theories, political scientists, like other scientists, must discover uniform relationships and account for nonconforming cases. Only in this way can they generalize as theory requires. Studies of foreign political systems are especially helpful in advancing these efforts, for they allow researchers to generalize more confidently. Some factors may seem related, although they are not, merely because they are connected with another factor which has been overlooked. Until 1958, for instance, French politics apparently demonstrated that a multiparty system produced executive instability. Persons familiar with Scandinavia knew this generalization was faulty, since the executive in these countries is very stable—the same man has been Prime Minister of Sweden for more than twenty years—even though many parties hold seats in the legislatures and one party rarely wins a majority. The overlooked factor was political consensus, which is high in Scandinavia but so low in France as to inhibit parties from cooperating durably and effectively.

An apparent relationship is less likely to be spurious—due to accidental circumstances or unconsidered intervening factors—if it can be found in several political systems. The same factors or characteristics are unlikely to occur together simply by coincidence in several environments. Gathering data from several systems also helps to reduce the possibility that the same intervening variable will continue to be present to mislead the researcher. Thus, accumulating a number of studies on the same topic in various countries helps to substantiate political theories by demonstrating that they are valid cross-nationally.

These studies must be comparable, however, if they are to be utilized effectively for this purpose. And when each researcher studies a single country, the comparability of their results is questionable. Do they reach different conclusions because the objects of their study really differ, or because they used different research techniques, or examined different data, or asked different questions? If a study of one system does not mention finding a particular relationship reported in a study of a second system, does it mean that the relationship doesn't exist in the first system, or merely that the first researcher didn't look for it?

The point of these questions is that political scientists can be more confident that discovered relationships really are valid cross-nationally if they are the result of a study which examines more than one country. The field of comparative politics requires comparative analysis, not parallel description. Unfortunately, although the number of comparative studies is increasing, they remain less typical than studies focusing on some aspect of a single foreign political system.

Studies of the latter type may be comparative, however, if they are replicative studies. A replicative study uses a previous study's research methods in attempting to reproduce the same results. Thus, since both studies are carried out in the same way, the replicative study indicates whether the original study's findings are valid for more than one country and may permit cross-national generalization.

A student familiar with the physical sciences will be surprised to learn that replicative studies, despite their value, are uncommon in political science research. Unlike physical scientists, political scientists seldom repeat an "experiment" to check the validity or ascertain the scope of their results. If they are skeptical of a study's findings, they may challenge the researcher's logic, his research design, or his interpretation of the results. They may attempt to disprove the findings by conducting their own study using different methods. Rarely will they investigate the subject in exactly the same way as did the study they question to see if they can obtain the same results. In most cases, therefore, no one knows whether the findings of political science are reproducible —the quality deemed essential for acceptance as established fact in the physical sciences.

This deficiency can be partially explained by the fact that political science studies are not usually experimental. In most instances political scientists simply cannot manipulate people, structures, and events to duplicate a previous situation. Nonetheless, they have not been sufficiently concerned with re-examining research findings; they almost seem to believe that the status quo is immutable. The conclusions of a major study are often treated as though they were valid perennially. If someone proposes another study on the same topic, the response often is, "That's already been done." More than fifty years passed, for example, after a thorough study of the power structure of British political parties was published in the early 1900s before anyone felt the subject worthy of another detailed analysis, despite the fact that during those years the British electorate almost sextupled, one major party declined to a more party, and another party rose from two seats in the House of Commons to more than 60 percent of the seats.

A further obstacle to replicative studies is their lack of prestige. They are treated as though they either smacked of plagiarism or demonstrated that their practitioners lacked minds sufficiently inventive to devise their own research problems and techniques. As a result, researchers attempt to prove their originality by giving a distinctive twist to studies that could have been replicative, thereby destroying much of their comparability.

Comparative studies, whether replicative or simultaneously analytical of more than one system, help both to strengthen political scientists' confidence that discovered relationships are not merely accidental, and to specify, by accumulating data from additional instances, the conditions in which discovered regularities hold. A political scientist needs not only to establish a political regularity's form empirically; he must also formulate a supportive logical theory to explain why the discovered regularity takes its particular form. When both tasks are completed, then, unsophisticatedly stated, the evidence of eye and of brain confirm each other.

Thus, comparative studies are essential to building political theories that are not only intellectually satisfying but also useful in improving political structures and processes. The results of a survey of more than 400 professional political scientists attested to the value comparative politics research is recognized to have for the advancement of political science. When their negative and favorable evaluations of the quality of work being done in the various fields of political science were balanced, comparative government ranked first of the seven fields in the discipline.[1]

An Approach to Political Analysis

Once you grant the importance of studying comparative politics, your next logical question is: How shall I go about it? For the advanced student planning a career in political science, this is a question about research strategies. What data are worth gathering? What means of analysis are likely to prove most fruitful? For other students, the frankly more relevant question is: Of all the material covered in a comparative politics course, which is worth remembering when the exams are over?

The quality that makes politics momentous provides a guide for distinguishing the significant from the trivial. Given government's monopoly of legitimate, publicly applicable sanctions, the obvious question is: Who possesses this power? who governs? by what means? for what purposes? This is what political science seeks to discover. Any information which helps you to answer these questions with greater understanding is worth retaining after you have completed the course. But information rapidly becomes outdated. Even students without a professional interest in political science need at least a study guide if not a research strategy. Such a guide is perhaps the most important knowledge you can acquire in a comparative politics course, for it can enable you subsequently to derive some meaning from the mass of political information spewed forth in books, magazines, newspapers, and news broadcasts.

Any research technique or analytical approach that aids in discovering who governs, by what means, and for what purposes is valuable. Individuals differ in the method they find most congenial to their tastes. I will discuss briefly some possible approaches and then develop a bit more fully one approach that I feel can be especially useful. Although I have a preference, I am not saying that all other approaches are worthless. Even more important than the approach chosen to study politics is the way in which that approach is applied. Political science has suffered not so much from inadequate approaches as it has from lack of rigor and thoroughness. If hypotheses are explicitly stated and operationalized, and all the relevant evidence is examined so that the hypotheses are tested rather than merely supported by selected example (which is not verification at all), the findings are likely to be valuable regardless of the approach employed.

Students of politics traditionally studied legal institutions; they examined, for example, the provisions of constitutions. How did the legal powers of the American President compare with those of the French President? This arid approach yielded few significant insights into politics and even tended to mislead comparative research by suggesting similarities which in fact did not exist.

Almost invariably a comparative study of legislative institutions examined both the American Congress and the British Parliament, although the roles of these two institutions in their societies' process of making authoritative rules differ fundamentally. The President can influence Congress considerably; yet Congress, not the President, effectively decides what laws shall be enacted in what form. In Britain, however, the Cabinet proposes virtually all the laws—few are initiated by legislators—and Parliament almost invariably not only passes these proposals but does so in a form agreeable to the Cabinet. The Cabinet's bills are not bottled up in committee; they are not mutilated by amendments. Clearly the Cabinet, not Parliament, determines what the authoritative rules shall be in Britain. Studying both Congress and Parliament as members of the same class—legislatures—suggests nonexistent similarities of power and purpose.

Focusing on legal institutions also excessively restricted the scope of research. Political power is not limited to the formal organs of government. Yet, only after muckraking exposés denounced parties and interest groups for debasing the governmental process by employing pressures and emotions rather than logical arguments based on facts, did students of politics perceive that they could not hope to understand adequately who governs if they ignored political organizations simply because they had not been established by law.

Salutary as was this broadening of the study of politics, it did not eliminate another major deficiency of the institutional approach—the tendency for institutional studies, whether concerned with legal or with extralegal institutions, to be more descriptive than analytical, more solitary than comparative. Even studies including more than one country usually just recounted the circumstances prevailing in first one political system and then another. What was missing was an integrated set of research concepts, an analytical framework, to interrelate data in the most meaningful, the most explanatory, fashion. Without such a framework, comparative studies are virtually impossible, for a researcher can only place profiles of his subjects side by side to see if they appear to match. With such a framework he sifts all his data through the same sieve in search of a common interrelated residue; he compares thoroughly, more directly, for he is analyzing multiple subjects simultaneously in the same fashion rather than describing them sequentially. Thus, his work is more likely to reveal essential relations and regularities.

Broadening the institutional approach to include extralegal bodies, however, has clarified the varied aspects of governing. Understanding who governs by what means for what purposes was rather more complicated than it appeared. Not only the

President and Congressmen, but judges, bureaucrats, party leaders, lobbyists, newspapers, and voters, to name only some, governed to various extents in diverse ways, ways that differed frequently in the United States from those in Britain, France, or other systems.

Yet underlying this diversity are certain similarities.[2] All political systems, be they dictatorial or democratic, modern or primitive, serve the same basic purpose—to determine authoritatively how to utilize a society's resources. Fundamentally similar conduct occurs, fundamentally similar tasks are performed in all continuing systems during this process.

The potentially most fruitful approach to the study of comparative politics, therefore, is to focus not on institutions but rather on activities and functions. In what ways, through what structures, are basic political functions performed in different societies and how do these differences affect political activity? To speak of structures is not to smuggle legal institutions back into political analysis under an alias. Structure is a broader concept meaning a system (an entity whose parts are interdependent) of roles (modal behavior patterns associated with particular posts or status). On the other hand, to study structures is not to ignore legal institutions. Many roles have a legal foundation or origin. Structural analysis simply recognizes that the behavior of and relations between political actors and organs is much more complex than a mere knowledge of legal provisions would suggest. The club atmosphere of the United States Senate may restrain a Senator considerably from opposing vigorously a policy or procedure which he knows a majority of his colleagues favor.

Although all political functions and activities are inextricably intwined—do, in fact, constitute a system—they should be distinguished intellectually to facilitate analysis.

In every political system people express their interests to, and make demands upon, government, for everyone wants authoritative decisions to be as congenial to him as possible. Admittedly, the government of dictatorial regimes restricts this activity considerably, yet it occurs even in these systems. Evidence available for both the Soviet Union and China amply demonstrates that dictatorial systems are not as monolithic as might be thought. Leaders of various power centers, like the army, the bureaucracy, the party, and the police, pursue divergent goals. Furthermore, whether they intend to repress or concede demands, even dictatorial leaders need to be aware of desires strongly or widely held in their societies.

The individual may express desires in a variety of ways; he may write them in a diary, mumble them to himself, discuss them with his spouse. He may become so frustrated by his inability to satisfy his desires that he joins others in an anomic outburst of senseless destruction, such as the riot in Watts, California. These largely inarticulate, directionless expressions of desires are not likely to be very effective. Mob action is difficult to interpret in terms of specific policies. The mob itself doesn't know its goals other than a generalized demand for improvement of an intolerable life. Admittedly, widespread and repeated mob action may motivate those who control political power to respond in ways which may placate the mob. When such behavior becomes the principal way of expressing demands, however, the established procedures for settling conflicts of interest authoritatively are clearly being repudiated, and the political system is on the verge of collapse.

Normally, then, you must go through channels, if your interests are to be politically relevant. You may use a channel that allows you to act individually—writing a letter to your Congressman or voting in an election. You are more likely to obtain a satisfactory response, though, if you act together with others through structures which direct the combined pressure of many individuals upon those points where it is most likely to be effective. Such structures help to focus the diffuse desires of mass society into a limited number of demands for authoritative action, thereby increasing the possibility of rational choice of alternatives. A political system whose structures fail to fulfill this function will probably not be effective. In Fourth Republic

France, for example, interests were highly fractionalized. Political parties tended to express the demands of narrow segments of society rather than to combine a number of interests. Thus they did little to limit the number of alternatives among which government had to choose. No effective executive could be constructed on the shifting foundation of a fissiparous parliament.

The structures through which interests are expressed and focused are not mere conveyors, transmitting demands to the government. Rather, they are filters or molds. Parties and interest groups will almost certainly modify the demands of any one member by combining those with the demands of the other members. Furthermore, the interests of the leaders of such organizations may differ from those of the followers; their desire to perpetuate the organization simply to maintain their own status may reduce the zeal with which they pursue the organization's professed goals.

Elections might seem to be an exception, a structure through which you can express your interests unalloyed. Yet they also channel demands. Write-in campaigns, even where legal, are rarely significant; your choice is restricted to the candidates on the ballot, although none of them may appeal to you.

Elections also modify the demands expressed through them because the meaning of the results is never apparent. The variety of issues discussed in a campaign, and the diversity of motivations for voting, refute effectively the old belief that an election can give a party a mandate for a specific policy. In 1945 the British Labour Party won a majority of almost 150 seats over all their opponents, yet their claim to have a mandate for nationalization of the iron and steel industry was questionable. Public-opinion polls indicated that a majority of the population, including a good number who had voted for Labour, did not favor nationalization. The voters had repudiated the Conservatives' callousness toward economic hardship in the 1930s and their appeasement of Hitler and Mussolini; they were attracted by Labour's image of social reform. They were not demanding nationalization. Election results are interpreted differently by different observers; the demands you express through this structure are necessarily modified in being focused.

The structures through which demands are transmitted or, more typically, transmuted, are also generators. They may stimulate new demands by suggesting to some individuals that they are deprived in ways in which they had not been aware.

This discussion suggests a number of questions for study. How do the structures available for expressing and focusing demands differ from one political system to another, and how does this difference affect the political process? How do the strategy and tactics which different structures employ in different systems vary? Demands for governmental action obviously must be expressed differently in the Soviet Union from the way they are expressed in the United States. The process in unitary, parliamentary Britain differs from that in federal, congressional United States. Are some structures more successful than others in obtaining governmental decisions to satisfy the demands expressed through them and, if so, why? Do some of these structures transform individual demands more than others? Are some organized so as to serve leaders' interests primarily and to attentuate followers' influence and control?

Government responds to the demands focused upon it by prescribing how much of its society's resources shall be spent to satisfy which demands. These prescriptions are not self-executing. To be effective rather than merely formal, they must be applied to concrete cases and the resultant disputes must be settled.

Who makes these authoritative decisions? Who prescribes? Who implements? If a political system were small enough, the citizens themselves might perform these functions. Yet even in Andorra (population 6,000) and San Marino (population 17,-000), political roles are specialized, differentiated; only part of the population is recruited into the authoritative processing of demands. Even apart from considerations of size, modern government deals with such complex problems that it must employ professionals who can devote full time to political affairs. Modern government is regent government. To discover who governs, we must study how these regents are chosen and from what segments of the population, and the extent to which their goals coincide with those of the rest of society.

Understanding how demands are processed is fully as important as knowledge of who processes those demands. Do some governmental structures prescribe and implement more expeditiously than others? Can social ailments be remedied more readily in Britain, where the power to prescribe is concentrated relatively, than in the United States, where it is more dispersed? How does concentrating prescriptive power affect freedom and popular control of the government? Are structures which process demands readily accessible for everyone—for Negroes in the southern United States? for Protestants in Spain? for nonparty members in the Soviet Union? To what extent do structures which are to implement prescriptions alter them and thus prescribe as well as implement? Will the country attorney, for example, refuse to prosecute local bookies and thereby in effect repeal the law prohibiting gambling? These are some of the leading questions to be answered about the structures which process demands for authoritative decisions.

Whether a political system processes demands efficiently, and prescribes and implements them effectively, depends in part on whether the system is stable. When personnel and structures are transient, governing can be little more than spasmodic. Stability is important for freedom as well as for efficiency. If authoritative rules can be altered by caprice, rather than by established procedures, freedom is jeopardized. If the rules of a game change while the game is being played—if in one inning the catcher is allowed to tackle the batter and in the next a baserunner is allowed to score from first without touching second and third—few people would desire or, for that matter be able, to participate.

Since the world is not static, however, a political system must be both flexible and stable. It must not be so rigid that it cannot adapt to change; paradoxically, a flexible political system may be more stable in the long run. A political system must be able to cope with an economic crisis, as the United States was able to weather the Depression without destruction of our political system. It must be able to adjust to social crises, as we now are doing in trying to accommodate Negro demands for equality. It must be able to contain political conflicts within the existing channels for settlement. In the nineteenth century the French political system failed to respond satisfactorily to demands for expanded suffrage; as a result the constitutional monarchy collapsed in 1848 and was replaced by a republic. Britain, on the other hand, successfully processed similar demands by extending the franchise gradually over almost a century. The British system was able to adapt to changes in its environment; the French system was not.

The contrasting political cultures of those two countries help to explain the different results. Political culture is the sum of individual evaluative attitudes toward the political system and conceptions of individual political behavior. The French, influenced by a culture which accepted nonconstitutional and violent means of political change as legitimate and which doubted the efficacy of gradualism, wanted complete reform at a single stroke and had no qualms about destroying the existing political system to get it. The British, who were more pragmatic and whose political culture valued evolutionary rather than revolutionary change, were willing to proceed gradually. Had its political culture been no more supportive than was the French, the British system might have collapsed under demands for a broadened franchise.

The ability of a political system to adjust to changes in the environment is affected by the degree of its members' loyalty. Are they committed to maintaining the existing system? Will they defend it against challenges? In January 1958 an opinion survey found that a majority of Frenchmen would do nothing if a coup were attempted, and only four percent would actively oppose it. It is no surprise that the Fourth Republic crumbled under the threat of a military insurrection and was supplanted by the Fifth Republic before the year ended.

An individual's commitment to maintaining the political system in which he lives does not depend simply upon whether the government grants all his demands. Just as demands are modified in being communicated to the government, so authoritative decisions are filtered in being transmitted to the individual. In assessing decisions, he will be considerably influenced by the reactions of various political groups to those decisions. Furthermore, he may accept distasteful decisions that have been legitimated, reached in conformity with established procedures. Even people whose demands are infrequently satisfied may be committed strongly to continuing to pursue their interests through the existing political channels, if the political culture teaches them that the existing political system is just and emphasizes gradual, peaceful means of change.

Therefore, developing a supportive political culture is clearly one of the major tasks of governmental leaders. Can the French and Italian governments convince the 20 to 25 percent of their electorates who regularly vote Communist that this behavior only weakens the government's ability to perform its functions effectively and seriously jeopardizes its ability to weather a major political or economic crisis? Can they rectify their political cultures' condoning, even encouraging, cheating tax collectors and devising schemes to circumvent the law?

Politicizing—the implanting of society's political culture in new members of that society—is not synonymous with propagandizing. The values transmitted may be subversive rather than supportive of the political system; they may be communicated unintentionally as well as deliberately. Fourth of July addresses and school historical pageants consciously seek to inculcate political values. Athletic contests, on the other hand, usually have no political purpose, yet students of British politics sometimes suggest that the belief that certain behavior "isn't cricket" restrains the British from violating political norms as well as athletic rules.

Nor, as these examples indicate, are governmental institutions the only, or even the most significant, politicizing structures. The failure of democracy in Germany in the 1930s has been charged in part to the authoritarian nature of the German family, which implanted attitudes hostile to a democratic political system.

Attitudes toward the political system and conceptions of how an individual should behave politically are communicated in dictatorships as well as in democracies. Hostile, yet cowed, attitudes may be transmitted within the population. The government may attempt to instill fear of its power and mutual distrust among its subjects. Or it may seek to convince them that it actually rules in their best interests. Spending scarce resources to repress a population is wasteful; rulers can more easily and efficiently control people in whom values supportive of the system have been instilled. Since the death of Stalin, the leaders of the Soviet Union have relied less on terror and violence, preferring to win, rather than coerce, support. This change in strategy suggests the limited effectiveness of repressive measures.

Political culture's significance lies not only in its relevance to political change. It is the context, the atmosphere, which conditions the performance of all the structures within a political system. In a society whose political culture emphasizes political equality, leaders may consult more frequently with followers, may try harder to share power with them, than they would in a society whose political culture stressed deference to experts. Political cultures which value liberty and freedom may generate groups like the American Civil Liberties Union, whose purpose is not the usual one of defending its members' immediate interests, but rather is of supporting anyone whose political freedom is jeopardized. Whether substantial numbers of people actively participate in politics or passively accept authoritative decisions varies considerably according to the way their society's political culture conceives the role of the good citizen.

To summarize briefly, members of all societies demand that their needs and wants be satisfied. These diverse demands are channeled through structures which focus them on the government because government's function is to allocate authoritatively the society's limited resources. In addition to its chief function, each of these structures has also the task of recruiting personnel to perform its activities. In order to endure, a system must process demands efficiently even though their number and urgency increase sharply; it must be sufficiently flexible to adapt to changes in its environment, yet sufficiently stable to keep change within the bounds of established procedure. Conditioning all these activities are the attitudes of the people toward politics and the political system.

This is the political scientist's province; these are the structures and processes he investigates in search of regularities and relationships; these are the phenomena he analyzes to explain his discoveries so that he may understand more fully the political aspect of man's life and thus help to make existence purposive and rational rather than merely one damned thing after another.

In this book I try, by summarizing and synthesizing some of the most significant findings of empirical comparative studies, to chart the basic landmarks in the discipline of political science. Unfortunately, many of these landmarks are not firmly established. Although they are supported by some evidence, they are no more than tentative findings or hypotheses, and thus may eventually be refuted. Those landmarks which survive are likely to be refined, to be made more precise, by subsequent research. Yet they serve as a foundation or guide for further study and thought in comparative politics. They can help to put studies of individual countries in perspective by distinguishing their unique from their common characteristics. This, then, is a partial and preliminary answer to the basic political inquiry: Who governs by what means for what purpose?

expansionist, while tyrannies, being the bad guys, are always megalomaniacs who threaten everyone—"Today, Germany; tomorrow, the world!"

This belief is erroneous. As the Spanish-American War demonstrates, democracies can be imperialistic. The largest empire in history—the British—culminated in a century in which the British constitutional monarchy was evolving toward mass democracy. On the other hand, although Spain has been rather nasty recently to Britain about Gibraltar, one hardly suspects Franco of plotting to take over Western Europe. The argument that democracies can get along better with each other than with dictatorships, because democracies share similar basic values and procedures for settling disputes, is an appealing argument. Yet the United States and de Gaulle's France have not been bosom allies. The thought that these disagreements might lead to war is absurd, but the War of 1812 illustrates that conflict between nontyrannical systems can go even that far.

Perhaps, then, Americans should be indifferent to the incidence of democracy. But we aren't; we have a *noblesse oblige* attitude toward the domestic political arrangements of the rest of the world. When we entered the First World War, many Americans were convinced that we did so to make the world safe for democracy. The same appeal, properly reburnished, serves forty years later to justify our action in Vietnam. The desire that others should also enjoy democracy remains robust; however, the doubt that they may not be able to do so also flourishes.

Are certain conditions prerequisite for a successful democracy? Was the attempt to implant a perfect democracy in Germany after the First World War really impractical idealism, doomed to fail from the start because Germany did not offer a fertile soil for democracy? Is it delusory to expect democracy to function effectively in the recently independent countries? Perhaps the real surprise is not that Nigeria collapsed to a coup within a coup in 1966, but that parliamentary government had endured for six years after independence.

Interest in such questions is justifiable apart from normative concerns. Government does not function in a vacuum; comparative politics studies neither utopias nor laboratory specimens, but concrete political systems embedded in specific historic, social, economic, geographic, and cultural contexts. That this environment should have no effect upon a political system is inconceivable. Political science must investigate environment's political impact to understand the variety of patterns of governing. Furthermore, only when political scientists have discovered what is possible within given conditions can they usefully propose to modify a political system.

Both world wars, the first by fostering the idea of national self-determination and the second by weakening the major colonial powers' control over their empires, helped to multiply the number of independent countries. Apart from outraging extreme conservatives in the United States (who bristle at the thought that the United States has no greater voting power in the United Nations' General Assembly than the Maldive Islands with its population of 94,000, but are undismayed that California has the same number of Senators as Arizona), this development raises a legitimate inquiry as to what conditions or characteristics are requisite to a viable, independent political system. Certainly the personnel of the British Colonial Office must have pondered this question frequently after the Second World War, as Britain divested herself of her empire. Colonists as well as colonizers may recognize that political fission must be limited if the resultant systems are to flourish; in 1966 some of Britain's territories in the Caribbean chose to remain "associated" with Britain rather than to press on for complete independence.

Although it is foolish to expect that countries must be self-sufficient to be self-governing (Britain, as well as India, would starve unless it imported food), it seems reasonable to believe that a minimal level of economic development is essential to sustain independence. Available evidence, however, questions this belief.[1] Economic development measured in terms of energy, steel, and food production, health standards, level of education, proportion of population living in urban areas, and extent of transportation and communications media, is related to self-government, as the table demonstrates. The most economically developed political systems are almost certain to be independent, while the least developed are more likely to be dependent than self-governing. Many of the least developed systems, however, are self-governing; in fact, a self-governing system is as likely to be among the least developed as among the most developed.

Size—either area or population—is more nearly essential, as can be seen from the table. Few self-governing countries have populations under 1,200,000 or are smaller than 20,000 square kilometers (about the size of Massachusetts), although, again, there are exceptions. Although size is related to self-government more closely than is economic development, size does not predict sovereign status with complete accuracy. Several of the larger political systems, especially the territorially larger, are not self-governing; the dependent systems are almost as likely to be over 20,000 square kilometers as they are to be under that size.

ECONOMIC DEVELOPMENT RELATED TO SOVEREIGN STATUS

	Self-governing systems	Dependent systems	Total
Most developed systems	28	1	29
Least developed systems	28	56	84
Total	56	57	113

POPULATION RELATED TO SOVEREIGN STATUS

	Self-governing systems	Dependent systems	Total
Over 1,200,000	71	27	98
Under 1,200,000	17	83	100
Total	88	110	198

AREA RELATED TO SOVEREIGN STATUS

	Self-governing systems	Dependent systems	Total
Over 20,000 square kilometers	80	50	130
Under 20,000 square kilometers	8	60	68
Total	88	110	198

In other words, you cannot distinguish independent from dependent political systems simply by classifying them according to economic development, population, or area. Although all these factors are related to self-government, none of them is requisite. A weakness in this conclusion is the fact that the evidence just discussed merely characterized those political systems which happened to be self-governing at the time of the study. Some of these systems had been independent for only a short time and might degenerate into civil war and anarchy, as the Congo did. Even if such a system remains independent, most people would hesitate to term it a viable system.

Thus, the conclusion the evidence warrants is: Neither small size nor limited economic development has prevented political systems from seeking and obtaining independence. Whether this behavior is wise, whether small, little developed systems can prosper, is another matter. The number of African systems interested in some form of federation or trade association with other African nations suggests that they are finding their recently established territorial boundaries too restrictive to solve some of their most pressing problems. (On the other hand, the conflict between Nigeria and Biafra suggests that political fission in Africa may not have been arrested yet.) This discovery is not limited to Africa; a number of Latin American countries have been exploring the possibilities of some form of trade association, and economic integration has proceeded furthest, of course, in Western Europe's Common Market.

Perhaps these developments presage a new trend in international relations. The political fission which has characterized
the first half of the twentieth century may have culminated, to
be replaced by a period of fusion like that of the mid-nineteenth
century when Italy and Germany were unified. Regardless of
this possibility, the evidence presented on the relation between
sovereign status and size and economic development is best interpreted as illustrating the strength of nationalism thus far in this
century; people feeling a national identity have sought their own
independent country despite the obvious debits of this goal in
many cases.

Nationalism confounds the attempts to discover the characteristics essential for self-government; it need not prevent the
search for democratic requisites. Granted that a political system
can become independent however unfavorable its circumstances,
what are its prospects for being democratic? In the middle of
the twentieth century the odds are not favorable. Democracy is
atypical; its image is that of a not-very-hardy hothouse plant
which can thrive only when cultivated most meticulously. Therefore, rather than condemning the many undemocratic countries
of the world for their shortcomings, it is preferable to attempt
to determine whether certain environmental conditions are essential, as demonstrated by their being associated regularly with
democracy, for democracy to exist.

A factor popularly thought necessary for democracy, especially
in articles on foreign aid, is economic prosperity and development. The reasoning that supports this belief is not difficult to
understand. When economic conditions are so bad that life is
primarily a struggle for survival, constitutional niceties attract
little interest. Politics is more visceral; defeat, even compromise,
is unacceptable. The American Medical Association vigorously
fought the passage of Medicare, but the program will not turn
doctors into paupers and, having been defeated through legitimate constitutional procedures, the doctors will manage to live
with it; they are not likely to man the barricades.

In a prosperous society, regardless of whether wealth is distributed equitably, some benefits are likely to filter down to even the most disadvantaged groups. Income is maldistributed almost as greatly in the United States as in Italy, yet the proportion of people alienated from the political system is much higher in Italy. In the more developed countries the proletariat has considerably more to lose than their chains. The world, or at least its material goods, has already been won. The advanced economy is characterized by a high level of education and well-developed communications media. These may help to increase interest in politics and expand the pool of those willing and able to participate in politics as officials or aware citizens. Clearly, economic conditions can contribute to democracy's success. As for historical evidence of this, the collapse of Germany's economy between the First and Second World Wars turned many people toward Hitler and destroyed the Weimar Republic.

Detailed studies on this topic have established that democracy, as well as self-government, is related to economic development.[2] Per capita wealth, level of industrialization and education, extent of urbanization, newspaper circulation, number of telephones and radios per capita—all these aspects of economic development help to distinguish democratic systems from dictatorial systems in particular areas.

The last qualifying phrase, which indicates the need to explore the popular belief more thoroughly, is added to account for the vast differences in economic level in different parts of the world. Lipset found that the average economic development of a group of thirteen European and English-speaking stable democracies exceeded that of a group of fifteen European unstable democracies and dictatorships and, similarly, that seven Latin American democracies and unstable dictatorships were on the average more developed economically than thirteen Latin American stable dictatorships; however, on most measures of economic development the European unstable democracies and dictatorships scored higher than the Latin American democracies and unstable dictatorships. Coleman's study of seventy-six Latin American, Asian, and African nations discovered the same relation. When the Latin American countries were grouped separately from the Asian and African countries, political competitiveness within each group varied directly with average economic development. On several measures, however, the average economic development of authoritarian Latin American nations surpassed that of competitive African and Asian nations.

The relation between democracy and economic development must be qualified still further. The method used to establish the relation was to group countries by political type and then to calculate the average score for the group on some measure of economic development. When the focus shifts from groups of countries to single nations, a number of deviant cases appear even within a single area. European democracies as a group are more developed than European dictatorships, yet East Germany and Czechoslovakia are more developed than is Greece.

The difficulty of separating nations into two or three types of political systems and levels of economic development also complicates the attempt to relate democracy to economic development. Development—economic or political—is best thought of as a continuum rather than as a series of discrete categories, for no definite "breaking points" exist to distinguish one type or level from the next. Brazil cannot be classified with, say, Switzerland, as a democracy, but neither can it be grouped under dictatorships along with the Soviet Union. Relegating all such cases to some type of residual "other" category is also suspect.

Such thoughts led Cutright to inquire whether degree, rather than type, of political and economic development are related. Instead of trying to cram the nations of the world into a few rickety pigeonholes, he ranked them in order of development to determine whether the most democratic was also the most developed economically and so on, through seventy-seven countries of North America, South America, Asia, and Europe.

Cutright also dealt with the problem of political change; instead of rating a country at a single date, he evaluated it over a twenty-one-year period. This more demanding test found that democracy and economic development are related even though countries are not grouped by geographical area. The economic development factor most closely associated with democracy is communications level as measured by proportion of telephones, newspaper and mail circulation, and newsprint consumption.

A drawback of Cutright's study is its narrow criteria for political development. Nations were scored only on whether their party system was competitive and on whether their procedure for selecting the chief executive involved the people even indirectly. Democracy needs to be defined more broadly. To do this I selected from Banks and Textor's *A Cross-Polity Survey* eight characteristics dealing with freedom of the press, constitutionalism, freedom of political association, political role of the military and of the police, representativeness and competitiveness of the electoral system, and competitiveness of the party system.[3]

On the basis of their scores on these characteristics I ranked 106 nations from most to least democratic. To obtain an index of economic condition I combined four characteristics—per capita Gross National Product, literacy rate, stage of economic development, and percentage of population in agriculture. The order in which the 106 nations ranked on the economic index was related to their position on the political spectrum. Although the two rankings are not associated closely, they are connected strongly enough to rule out the possibility of chance relation.[4]

However, the evidence discussed does not warrant considering economic development a democratic requisite. Not only are some economically developed nations not democratic, but some democratic nations have developed little economically. Instead of searching for democratic requisites—conditions without which democracy cannot exist—we would be better advised to try to specify factors which, although perhaps not essential for democracy's success, help to sustain it. An advanced economy can obviously do this. It can nurture, it can facilitate; more cannot be claimed.

Many Americans associate democracy with two other factors more closely than with economic development. They attribute the existence of democracy in the United States to the "free enterprise system" and, almost tautologically, to the Bill of Rights. The possibility that these are democratic requisites deserves brief comment.

Determining whether democracy is related to "free enterprise" is complicated by the difficulty of giving precise meaning to this vague term. If it means that business is unaffected by government, no country's economic system can qualify. All governments intervene in economic activity, at times to restrict business action, such as with the Pure Food and Drug Act, and at times to assist business, such as with the oil depletion allowance. Similarly, at the other extreme no government completely controls the economy; even the Soviet Union permits a substantial amount of "free enterprise" in goods grown on the peasants' garden plots. This is not a trivial instance; in 1960 half of the milk and meat and 80 percent of the eggs produced in the Soviet Union came from those "gardens."

The absence of government ownership is hardly a more satisfactory criterion for distinguishing a "free enterprise system." Government ownership is not uncommon even in the United States—the Tennessee Valley Authority, public waterworks, and municipal trash collection are examples. The Post Office should be cited as well, since there is no intrinsic reason why the business of mail delivery could not be left to private companies. The Pony Express carried the mail not as a government service, but to make a profit for Russell, Majors, and Waddell. The usefulness of government ownership as a distinguishing criterion is weakened further by the fact that Sweden, which in the United States is popularly conceived to be quite socialistic, has relatively little government ownership. Thus it is difficult to specify a set proportion of government ownership which would qualify an economic system for the label "free enterprise."

The point can be made, however, that government ownership can proceed much further than it has in the United States without jeopardizing democracy. Switzerland, Canada, Australia, and New Zealand are all unquestionably democracies and appear likely to remain such for the foreseeable future. Yet in all four the railroads and the communications system (radio, television, telephone, and telegraph) are owned totally or partially by the government. In the latter three, government also owns airlines, electricity industries, and central banks, and even this is not a complete list of government businesses in Australia and New Zealand. Although citing a few examples does not constitute a rigorous proof that the type of economic system is largely irrelevant to the type of political system, it does at least demonstrate that "free enterprise" is not requisite for democracy.

Since constitutional guarantees of freedom would seem to be an element of democracy almost by definition, surely they must be requisite. Americans' liberties are traceable to and protected by the United States Constitution. But this is not because constitutions inherently possess magical powers to shield people from tyranny. The United States Constitution protects liberties because it is effective, not merely formal or nominal. And it is effective chiefly because it is regarded as an enforceable set of obligations and limits upon the government's power. In most countries the purpose and function of a constitution are conceived of differently. Latin American constitutions tend to be statements of aspirations; they list goals to be attained in the future, rather than rights to be enjoyed in the present.[5] Similarly, in Italy parts of the 1948 constitution have yet to be implemented, such as the creation of a system of regional governments. Even such a routine matter as instituting the constitutional court, which interprets the constitution authoritatively, took eight years.

Some constitutions contain impressive catalogues of freedoms not because those who control the government intend the people to exercise these rights, but because government wants to create a facade to help fend off the odium which attaches to dictatorships. The constitution of the Soviet Union, whose writing Stalin supervised, provides for political equality, due process of law, and freedom of religion, speech, press, and assembly. In practice these provisions have been meaningless.

Liberty's prestige has sufficiently attracted many newly independent states so that they have written extensive lists of personal rights into their constitutions. For example, most of the constitutions of the fourteen former French African colonies which became independent between 1957 and 1961 committed their countries to both the French 1789 Declaration of the Rights of Man and the United Nations' General Assembly's 1948 Universal Declaration of Human Rights.[6] Yet in A Cross-Polity Survey Banks could classify only two of these nations as clearly constitutional systems.

If it is incorrect and even naive to suppose that a mere statement of rights, even in a constitution, can ensure that a system is democratic, can it at least be said that no democracy lacks such a statement? The most widely known negative case is Britain, which lacks even a written constitution, that is, a single framework document distributing political power and specifying procedures for reaching authoritative decisions. One of the several documents accorded constitutional status in Britain is a Bill of Rights. This is not an extensive list of individual freedoms, however; the guarantee of free speech applies only to parliamentary debates. Given their close historical ties with Britain, it is not surprising that Canada, Australia, and New Zealand lack constitutional guarantees of individual liberties even though they do have written constitutions. In these democracies freedom is founded on legal precedent and, even more important, on widely held political values.

Political Culture's Contribution to Democracy

It is platitudinous to say, in effect, that what really matters for democracy's success is that its values live in the hearts of the people. Recent research has confirmed, however, what until then had been little more than conjecture, and has specified clearly the political values and attitudes conducive to democracy. Democracies are more likely to be effective and stable when they have a self-confident citizenry.[7] The self-confident citizen is proud of his country's political institutions and moderately interested in politics. He feels relatively uninhibited about discussing politics. He believes that government action has a significant and generally beneficial effect on his life; he expects fair and considerate treatment from the police and bureaucrats; he believes people should participate in local community affairs, even if only passively by being informed and by voting.

In interviews with almost 5,000 people from the United States, Britain, Italy, Germany, and Mexico, Almond and Verba found that well over a majority—usually two-thirds or more—of the American and British respondents possessed the qualities described above, which generally were much rarer among interviewees from the three less well-established democracies.

There were two exceptions. One was that only 46 percent of the British, compared to 85 percent of the Americans, mentioned being proud of their political institutions. This was a substantially greater proportion, however, than those who took pride in political institutions in any of the three other countries and far outranked—over two and a half times as great—any other factor as a source of British national pride. The second exception was that only 48 percent of the Americans expected bureaucrats to consider their point of view seriously. Although this was lower than the proportion in Germany (53 percent), 83 percent of the Americans expected bureaucrats to treat them equally regardless of who they were, while only 65 percent of the Germans anticipated such treatment.

The only other case in which respondents from the less well-established democracies led Americans and Britons was in political information. Almond and Verba found some evidence to suggest that Germans are better informed politically than either Americans or Britons. Aside from these instances, the proportion of people possessing each of the attributes of the self-confident citizen was greater in the old, established democracies than in the three other nations.

The self-confident citizen is also less intensely hostile toward his political opponents—he does not let political differences produce social or personal enmity. He trusts others more than does the person who is not self-confident. And, most importantly, he believes that he is politically competent—that he can affect government action. The significance of this quality lies in the discovery that, in all five countries studied, those who feel politically competent are more likely to feel that democracy is desirable, to believe that people ought to participate in politics and to be politically active themselves, to gain satisfaction from voting, and to feel that governmental action improves conditions (this last attitude was not true in Mexico, however). Thus, those who feel competent are a primary source of support for a democratic system.

These findings are corroborated by other cross-national studies. From a survey of almost 1,400 manual workers in France and Italy, the occupational group from which these countries' Communist Parties draw their greatest support, Cantril found that more than 85 percent of the workers had little or no interest in politics.[8] They disparaged their country's political system and felt that the government was more likely to harm than help them. They felt ineffective and had little trust in others. Similarly, a study of former American, British, French, and Italian Communists revealed that neurotic hostility and isolation were fairly common characteristics (especially among the first two nationalities), which helped to explain why they joined the Communist Party.[9] Such people are obviously not self-confident citizens and it is precisely these people who are especially susceptible to an antidemocratic political movement.

Given the significant support a self-confident citizen can provide for democracy, the crucial question is: What produces such citizens? How can feelings of competence be instilled in a population? Characterizing the most important types of political cultures and processes provides a partial answer.[10]

An uncomplicated but useful taxonomy—a scheme for classifying that helps to group similar items together to reveal the patterns they have in common which distinguish them from other items—is for this purpose, one of two main categories, transitional and modern political systems, with the latter subdivided into coercive, fragmented, and consensual political cultures.[11] Such a fourfold scheme obviously oversimplifies reality. Not every country in the world can be classified readily under one of these labels and even those which can be fitted into one of the categories may not possess all the characteristics of that particular type. But every taxonomy, unless it includes a separate category for every item to be classified, oversimplifies to some extent. As long as the four categories suggested here are thought of as ideal types, to one of which most of the world's political systems generally correspond, they help to distinguish significant differences among various political systems.

The political culture of the transitional systems is a mixture of diverse elements. Since in many cases these nations' boundaries were drawn according to colonial powers' spheres of influence, rather than to more rational or "natural" factors, they may include several indigenous cultures in addition to that of the colonial ruler, or, perhaps, rulers. Furthermore, the efforts of these nations' leaders to modernize their countries and develop their economies have introduced modern elements into the traditional culture. These diverse subcultures may clash, as, for example, the Malayan and Chinese cultures did in Malaysia, leading eventually to the secession of Singapore from the federation, or they may coexist, having relatively limited impact on each other, with one culture dominant in the urban centers and another in the rural areas. Alternatively, feelings of rootlessness and directionlessness produced by the crumbling of traditional society from the challenges to the former eternal verities may culminate in a charismatic culture—one dominated by a leader whose aura of infallibility enables him to proclaim goals and values giving life some significance once again.

In addition to lacking a common value system, transitional political systems are little specialized or bureaucratized. Because life is not compartmentalized, politics is influenced by irrelevant —nonpolitical—factors. Social and personal relations and preferences determine political behavior. Instead of creating new specialized structures to process political demands, these systems channel demands through existing nonpolitical structures. Except in Latin American transitional systems, few groups are formed specifically to influence the government, and those which are tend to be ephemeral. The government's action is affected more by institutional interest groups, like the army and the bureacracy, and nonassociational interest groups, that is, groups which are formed for nonpolitical purposes and which intervene in politics only sporadically, like ethnic or tribal groups. The political division of labor has not proceeded very far. Political officials and structures perform a variety of functions. Military leaders frequently not only influence the government; they are the government.

Politics in these systems is more a spectator than a participatory sport. Following the intrigues of this exciting adventure may be entertaining; alternatively, observing the performance of its rituals may be comforting. Politics is not conceived of as a process for solving public problems by choosing from among several policy alternatives. This view is reflected in the character of political parties. Rather than being founded on a set of policy alternatives, they are either based on loyalty to a prominent personality or stand for a total way of life.

Such an all-encompassing purpose makes the ruling group's opponents, who have a comprehensive philosophy of their own, seem subversive. This is especially true in Asia and Africa, where the political leaders were associated first with the drive for independence and then with efforts to integrate their people into a unified, self-conscious, modernizing nation. (Since independence came considerably earlier for most Latin American nations, their nationalistic, modernizing movements are not associated with independence, as such movements are in Asia and Africa.)

These circumstances discourage thinking of government action as the result of debate among and accommodation of opposed interests; they stress instead the idea that it is the product of a unified national will. The nature of parties means that leaders are little restricted in their choice of policy and method. Leaders' past services and present nation-building goals, combined with the previously noted anxiety induced by a collapsing value system, help to produce charismatic leaders, whose authority is unchallenged. In these situations, the democratic concepts of responsibility and accountability are obviously irrelevant.

Before condemning the fervent, unquestioning obedience these leaders command, Americans should recall that many people wanted to make George Washington king after the Revolutionary War, and that in both 1789 and 1792 every Presidential elector voted for Washington. Even as late as 1820 James Monroe, who, unlike Washington, was not a charismatic leader, gained all but one of the electoral votes cast for President. In the early years of the United States, politics was frequently only the interaction of personal cliques and family groups just as it is now in many Asian, African, and Latin American nations.

The political culture of a modern system is also mixed; the modern system differs from the transitional, however, in being more specialized and bureaucratized. New structures are created specifically to handle political activity rather than to attempt to deal with it through existing structures. These new structures are durable and well-organized with their own established procedures. Relations are more impersonal; society is more conscious of rules. Not only are these secondary structures and relations more important in politics than are primary ones, but the secondary tend to modernize the primary. As social and political structures in the United States, for example, encourage people to participate more fully, family patterns became more participatory and less authoritarian. Of course, primary relations continue to have an important impact upon secondary relations even in a modern society, a point which will be developed more fully later.

The way in which the mixed elements of political culture are related, whether they are combined by coercion or consensus to form a unified culture or continue to clash with each other, distinguishes the three types of modern systems—coercive, fragmented, and consensual.

The coercive system is modern because its political structures and relations are specialized and bureaucratized. The coercive quality of the secondary level also tends to permeate primary structures and relations. Unlike transitional systems, authority is supported not by tradition or charisma (although this may be of some importance in the early stages of the coercive system), but rather by apathy and conformity. A single culture is imposed upon society; nonetheless, the coercive system retains some of the characteristics of the transitional. The modern system's bureaucratic, rational procedures are compromised by capricious penalties intended to terrorize, and thus control, the population.

Although specialized political structures exist in the coercive system, politics is no more a separate sphere of human activity than it is in transitional systems. In transitional systems, however, personal and social relations have precedence and encompass political relations, while in coercive systems political relations blot out all others. This is why these systems are labeled totalitarian; the political sphere is total. Their political philosophy proclaims that its values and goals must govern all behavior, since all—art, religion, recreation, or any other—has political content. Thus, in these systems as well as in the transitional, dissent is considered subversive. People may be encouraged to participate in some forms of political activity as a quasidemocratic ritual or facade, but they are not permitted to play a meaningful or effective role. Associational groups are usually prohibited or strictly controlled; institutional groups have the greatest influence on government policy.

Unlike the various subcultures in the traditional system, those in the modern fragmented system all have indigenous roots; each can claim to be the true culture. No unity has been imposed as in the coercive system, and voluntary procedures have failed to evolve a single set of widely acceptable values. Parties, therefore, tend in this system also to embody total ways of life. Politics has some of the attributes of a holy war as one faith clashes with another. Since so much is at stake, political participants are little inclined to compromise. Equally important, the political structures conflict with the culture. The modern, democratic structures of these systems are intended to facilitate bargaining between opposed interests as a means of accommodating their differing desires. A fragmented culture encourages not bargaining but exhortation and proselytizing; it encourages behavior that makes the system inoperable. Thus the political system fails to fulfill its function of resolving conflict. This may so disaffect many people that they become willing to accept a coercive system to unify the political culture synthetically and thus escape, at least temporarily, the fragmented system's stagnation.

The fragmented system is unlikely to produce many self-confident citizens. Political toleration is not common in such a system. The democratic norm of active participation continues to be challenged by some subcultures, and when coercive tendencies dominate, it is rejected entirely. Thus citizens are less likely to be certain that their proper political role is that of participant rather than that of merely subject.

In the consensual system, as the name suggests, voluntary agreement on political ends and means is widespread. The political culture is not homogeneous, but the mixed elements have been incorporated successfully so that the culture is fused rather than fragmented. Just as people in transitional systems feel that politics has no significance for their lives, so people in consensual systems also deny its relevance, but only to *some*, not all, aspects of life. In other circumstances people in consensual systems share the outlook of those in coercive systems; they obey the laws and follow the instructions of government officials. But the political experience of people in consensual systems is not limited simply to being passive recipients of governmental action; at other times they are initiators.

The virtue of the consensual culture is not, however, that it motivates people to participate, but that it manages to combine apolitical, subject, and participant roles in a balanced blend to produce a citizen role. It thus avoids the detrimental effects which each of these roles has in its pure form. Although the citizen knows that politics affects his life significantly, he sees its sphere as limited. Political activity is not an all-consuming passion for him; the residue of the transitional system's culture helps to save the consensual system from a surfeit of zealots committed to implementing a total way of life. Thus politics can be the pragmatic process of bargaining over alternative policies, rather than the proclamation of a mythical national will or a holy war over rival world views. The consensual system reconciles seemingly divergent cultural elements to produce a unified and functional, although mixed, culture.

Of the four main types of political systems just discussed, the modern, consensual system is clearly the one in which self-confident citizens are most likely to thrive. In such a system people have opportunities to participate meaningfully in political affairs in an atmosphere of social trust and toleration.

Social Factors Nurturing Self-confident Citizens

Factors other than the political system and its culture may help to produce self-confident citizens. Almond and Verba found that in all five of the countries they studied, more of those who belong to an organization—religious, social, business, or other —feel politically competent, than do those who are not members. Members of a political organization are even more likely to feel competent than members of a nonpolitical organization. And more active members than passive feel competent. Thus a pluralistic society contributes significantly to the politicizing of self-confident, democratic supporting citizens.[12]

It is questionable, however, whether vigorous group activity has another of the beneficial effects frequently claimed for it. Many political scientists have argued that politics is less likely to be extreme in a society that has a larger number of voluntary groups, because a person belonging to several groups will probably be exposed to divergent views. Such exposure helps to produce a willingness to compromise which is conducive to democracy. An individual comes to understand that issues have more than one side; new perspectives seem less outlandish to him.

Some of his contacts incline him to favor one course of action politically, while other contacts in other groups to which he belongs influence him in a different direction. In resolving these competing goals he comes to adopt a moderate stand on public issues. Leaders of political groups, aware that their followers are subject to such diverse pressures, tone down their demands upon government and other groups. Thus political conflict is partially settled before it reaches the structures empowered to make authoritative decisions. To this extent the clash of interests is less sharp, political tension is reduced, and people are more likely to trust their political opponents and less likely to respond violently to their successes.

This is the theory of cross-pressures. The logic of the theory demands that an individual's group memberships overlap. If they are cumulative, if they bring him in contact with people having the same views as his, they will tend to reinforce his beliefs and thus exacerbate, rather than moderate, political conflict by encouraging extremism and dogmatism.

Several studies have substantiated the usefulness of the theory of cross-pressures in explaining voting behavior; however, the hypothesis that cross-pressures encourage political tolerance has not been verified.[18] In Italy, where groups do not cut across subcultural lines, where group membership is cumulative, Verba found that people who belong to a number of groups are more hostile to opponents than those who do not, and that group officers are more hostile than members are. Although groups in the United States, in contrast, bring together people of different backgrounds and political preferences, and although group membership overlaps, Verba discovered no evidence that multigroup membership reduces political hostility or encourages group leaders to moderate their views.

Apparently, overlapping membership fails to have its anticipated effect in the United States because Americans are aware that the groups to which they belong include members whose political views differ from their own. They hesitate, therefore, to talk politics, so contrasting political ideas are not communicated despite overlapping membership. Thus, although cumulative group membership can worsen political conflict and thereby weaken democracy, overlapping membership does not necessarily aid democracy by increasing political tolerance. The fact that group membership is associated with a politically aware and active citizenry may be cause for concern; democracy will fare better when zealots participate less frequently in public affairs.

Almond and Verba discovered that in addition to members of groups, those more likely to feel politically competent include people who have been able to participate in family, school, and work decisions. In other words, the habit of participating is contagious. When a person's social relations make him feel that his opinions are valuable and can affect the decisions shaping his life, he naturally wishes to play the same role in political affairs. Of these three experiences, participating on the job seems to have the greatest impact, although it cannot make up entirely for having been denied a voice in school discussions and family decisions. But advanced education can compensate for these two deficiencies. Furthermore, feelings of political competence increase with education. In view of these findings, it is not surprising that French and Italian workers are not self-confident citizens. Not only are they poorly educated, but Cantril's survey, mentioned previously, uncovered evidence that they have little control over decisions affecting their work.

The importance of education in producing a political culture that emphasizes participant norms is evident in the effects which Almond and Verba found education has in the countries they studied. As the level of education rises, so also does the number of people interested in politics and aware of the government's impact on their lives. Fewer of those who are better educated are hesitant to talk politics, and in fact more of them do talk politics. With rare exceptions, greater education increases the proportion of people who expect fair and considerate treatment from police and bureaucrats. The more highly educated are more likely to belong to some organization, to believe that people should participate in local community affairs, and to feel that people can be trusted. Thus in the United States, Britain, Germany, Italy, and Mexico the more highly educated participate more fully in politics. Education tends to reduce national differences in political behavior; the better educated do not differ so much from one country to another as do the poorly educated.

Similarly, public-opinion polls in various countries have found that education increases support for democratic values and practices.[14] The better educated are more tolerant, less authoritarian. And those who are more tolerant tend to be better informed politically, more active in politics, and more often to be members of voluntary nonpolitical organizations.

Education's greatest impact is limited, however, to political awareness, social trust, and participation in political and nonpolitical activities. Political values appear to be only slightly affected by education and to be shaped much more significantly by national differences. Although the belief that one should participate in community affairs does increase with education, the difference between the well educated and the poorly educated is not great. Of the five countries included in *The Civic Culture*, only in the United States is extent of education in direct proportion to the number of people who regard forming a group a useful tactic for obtaining particular action from the government. And contrary to the data mentioned in the previous paragraph, Almond and Verba found that better-educated Germans, Italians, and even Britons were not especially more tolerant of their political opponents than were those of lower education. Nor did education overcome German and Italian lack of pride in their political systems or increase the number of people who gained satisfaction from voting. Perhaps this is simply another way of stating the obvious point that although education can contribute significantly to a democratic political culture, it does not guarantee that a country will be democratic. A high level of education did not prevent Germany from going Nazi, nor has it enervated Communism in the Soviet Union.

Nonetheless, the fact that education and democracy are strongly associated leads Lipset to contend that although a high level of education is not a sufficient condition, "it comes close to being a necessary condition" for democracy. This statement may be qualified sufficiently to be valid, but several contrary cases exist to challenge it. Measuring educational level in terms of literacy rate and newspaper circulation rate, I found that ten of the world's thirty-five most democratic countries (as ranked by their scores on the eight characteristics drawn from *A Cross-Polity Survey*, discussed previously) were not among the top thirty-six best educated. Half of these ten might be considered borderline cases, since their literacy rates were between 50 and 89 percent, although their newspaper circulation rates were low, ten to ninety-nine copies per thousand population. Yet it is hard to call these countries' level of education high. The other five countries ranked still lower, two even having literacy rates of under 10 percent and newspaper circulation rates of less than ten copies per thousand.

However, before rejecting Lipset's generalization because it holds in only 70 percent of the cases, two facts should be observed. Except for the Dominican Republic, which technically has been independent since 1865, these ten countries became independent after the Second World War; their median length of independence was in fact only three years at the time that data were collected for *A Cross-Polity Survey*. Of their number only the Philippines can claim to be a reasonably well-established and stable democracy, since political crises occur frequently in Ceylon and India, and none of the other countries had more than six years' experience as independent democracies. Since it is not certain that these are viable democracies, they may not refute the generalization that a high level of education is necessary for democracy. About a decade must pass before we will know how many really are deviant cases.

The second notable fact is that seven of these ten countries are former British possessions and one, the Philippines, is a former American possession. This fact suggests that these nations may have received special tutelage in democratic values and procedures which may have helped at least to create a political elite familiar with and favorable to democracy. Even the nonelite population is likely to have been given greater opportunity for and experience in self-government than it would have received in the Belgian Congo, for example. This historical experience which provided a training ground for democracy may help to overcome the lack of a high level of education; the sense of political competence productive of the self-confident citizen may have been implanted by means other than education.

This line of argument is supported by noting the type of political system most typical of former British possessions. Of the seventeen countries who were members of the Commonwealth, excluding Britain, when *A Cross-Polity Survey* was compiled, or had been British possessions, excluding the United States and South Africa (for which insufficient data was available to be ranked), only three were among the least democratic half of the world's nations (ranked in the fashion discussed previously) and twelve were among the thirty-five most democratic. Former British possessions were so much more likely than countries which were not British colonies to be among the world's most democratic nations, that it seems very unlikely that these two characteristics—former British possession and democratic political system—were unrelated. The fact that they were related is not a prediction, of course, that these countries will continue to be democratic and need not fear attempted coups, since many other factors are also relevant.

To summarize this chapter's discussion, democracies are most likely to succeed when their citizens are self-confident. Among the leading producers of such citizens are modern political systems with a consensual culture; a high level of education; numerous opportunities to participate effectively in social and personal relations; and membership in voluntary groups, especially active membership in political groups. Granted that these factors are conducive to a self-confident citizenry, how are they to be attained?

Economic development logically would seem to be one of the key instrumental processes, particularly since national wealth and democracy are related. Economic development not only requires better communications and education but also produces additional wealth so that more can be spent for these purposes. It both requires and produces an industrial labor force concentrated in urban areas. It provides a base for associational groups. Its search for efficiency requires specialized and bureaucratized structures. Economic development modernizes a society, and a modernized society is more favorable to democracy than is a traditional or a transitional society.

Yet a modernized society also has a greater potential for a totalitarian political system than does a traditional society. This is just one reason why only a political Pollyanna would expect the world's nations to become more democratic during the next century simply because they advance economically. We cannot be certain that prosperity and democracy will continue to be related. Even should they be, they are associated only statistically. The evidence I have reviewed in this chapter does not establish a causal relation or even reveal covariance. While a developed economy may be conducive to democracy, the process of modernizing the economy may not be. In the next chapter I will explore the ways in which political change is related to economic modernization.

Chapter 3

Varieties of Political Change

Obstacles to Evolutionary Studies

The attempt to relate definite stages of economic development to specific types of political systems is widely suspect in
political science, largely because most political scientists have
repudiated historicism in general and Karl Marx in particular.
The obvious futility of seeking fundamental causes that impel
all human behavior toward teleological goals apparent only to
the intellectual elite has made political scientists wary of evolutionary studies. The inability of Marx's theory—that political
systems must progress through predetermined stages of productive development on their inevitable route to the classless society
—to explain the Communists' seizure of power in Russia in
1917, dramatically demonstrated the inadequacies of the his-
toricist approach to political research.

Marx also exemplifies another failing of the historicists—the
tendency to offer monistic explanations, to believe that reality is
such an interrelated, organic whole that life can be analyzed in
terms of a single motivating force—for Marx, economics; for
Hegel, the World Spirit. Important as any of the factors might

be, the attempt to explain all history on that basis alone cannot help but yield an oversimplified analysis.

Even if the errors of the historicists are avoided by rechanneling such interests into a concern with political change—a less pretentious, more legitimate area of study—difficulties remain. To speak of stages of development or types of systems suggests distinct dividing points or characteristics that do not exist. Separating a continuous process of change into discrete categories must be arbitrary to some extent. Choosing the measures of development is a problem. An economy producing chiefly raw materials and agricultural goods can be distinguished easily from one whose main output is a broad variety of manufactured products requiring a sophisticated level of technology and a fairly high level of interdependence between economic units, both domestic and foreign. But specifying enough unique characteristics to create a typology of more than two or three categories is considerably more difficult.

Devising measures of political development is even harder. The growth of democracy is not a satisfactory index of political development; the Soviet Union's political structures have obviously progressed far beyond those of a tribal society, yet it is not a democratic system. Rating Czechoslovakia less modern now than it was in the 1920s is not very sensible. Measuring a political system's maturity in terms of the extent to which it has created structures specifically to perform a single political function is little better as an approach.

The argument seems to be that greater specialization and efficiency are hallmarks of modernity because they characterize a mass-production economy; why this justifies their use as measures of political development is not self-evident. Even if they are accepted as indices, they do not distinguish stages of political development as sharply as one might expect. The family is not a group created for political purposes; yet, as voting studies have shown, it significantly affects political behavior in the contemporary United States, thereby playing a political role. The Federal Bureau of Investigation was created to detect and apprehend criminals, not to form policy. At times, however, it is involved in the making of even foreign, to say nothing of domestic, policy, as for example when the Senate was considering the US-USSR consulary treaty in 1967. Despite being part of a modern or developed political system, American political structures are commonly multifunctional.

Problems like these counsel caution in studying political and economic change; they should not preclude such study. The great majority of the world's countries are attempting to industrialize and diversify their economics. These efforts cannot help but have political impact. Economic change has what might be called a spillover effect. Its impact cannot be retained behind the dikes of a water-tight economic sphere. Rather, it flows through society altering social, political, religious, and artistic, as well as economic, processes, values, and structures.

Since we cannot manipulate whole nations in a grand social experiment to discover the effects of economic change, the only alternative (unless we are to regard the whole process as merely a series of fortuitous surprises—hardly an attitude likely to deepen our understanding) is to examine the experience of those countries which have already passed through this process. Can patterns of concomitant change suggestive of interrelated political and economic development be discovered? If so, do they clarify and elaborate the previously established association between an advanced economy and democracy? Do some changes in the economic system help to limit political power or to distribute it more widely?

To focus on such questions is not to imply that democracy is the most mature or the most modern political system, the wave of the future which will sweep over the entire world. Nor is the purpose of these questions to predict the future of the developing countries. Rather, the objective is to formulate hypotheses that will guide further research on political and economic change especially, but not solely, in developing countries. Such hypotheses spare the researcher the burden of digging up the entire countryside in search of artifacts and permit him instead to begin his work on a burial mound. They help him to distinguish the common from the unique and thus to know which of his findings are unexplained and require further research.

Political and Economic Development in Industrially Advanced Nations

Modern national political development did not begin until the transient, largely personally based political loyalties of the feudal period were superseded within a limited geographical area, at least among the holders of power and influence, by more permanent feelings of political community.[1] Common language, natural geographical boundaries, and similar customs were among the factors contributing to a greater sense of national consciousness or national identity. To encourage the growth of such feelings—to build a nation—was the initial, basic political task of national leaders. They may have done this by providing a service, such as settling disputes by dispensing justice through national agents on the basis of an increasingly uniform national law. Or they may have encouraged distinctive national sentiments by waging war against other peoples and obtaining new territory to enhance the prestige and attractiveness of the nation. Specific techniques varied from one country to another.

Structures helpful in creating a unified nation were a military force and a bureaucracy which were professional and centrally responsible. The prospects for both democracy and economic development were better, however, if the military and the bureaucracy were relatively ineffective and unreliable. Then the central government had to court, rather than coerce, obedience; its power was not unlimited and the practice of seeking assent for authoritative action was implanted. A strong navy did not hinder greatly these developments, for it little augmented the monarch's power to dominate his domestic opponents. But a powerful army obviously allowed him to impose his will, as did a centralized bureaucracy whose members functioned as direct agents of the monarch. More conducive to the growth of democracy was a largely autonomous bureaucracy whose members merely cooperated in executing central government decisions, who had to be requested, rather than commanded, to act.

During the nation-building period, the negative effect of a strong, centralized bureaucracy on the development of democracy is easy to understand; why it also retarded economic development is less obvious. Detailed central control over the economy —mercantilism—would seem more effective logically than unplanned development in attaining rapid economic growth. This was not the case, however, for countries which began industrializing in the nineteenth century. Although the economic units in decentralized economies lacked perfect information, they had no need for it. At the pre-industrial stage of economic development, economic units had little effect on each other; thus, gathering more information before acting could not help them to behave more rationally. Not only was a centralized economy not necessary, therefore; it proved to be a definite liability. Poor communications meant that information available centrally was considerably out-of-date and likely to be more inaccurate, having been garbled in transmission, than when it had been gathered. The effort to attain more perfect economic information resulted in greater misapprehension of the true situation. Not surprisingly, therefore, the national government of a centralized system was likely to issue economic orders which were either wrong or mistimed.

Whether a monarch was sufficiently dominant to obtain centralized control over a nation, or whether he had to share power with a strong aristocracy in a more decentralized system, seems to be fortuitous. In the late medieval and early modern periods the monarch's forces won in some countries and lost in others. Changes in the balance of power did not, of course, follow a straight line in any country. At times the monarch's power might be eclipsed only to shine forth later with renewed glory. So contentiously did the aristocracy strive in some instances for royal preferment that they destroyed all feelings of class solidarity; mutual suspicions arose which precluded collective resistance to the monarch. Why the conflict should have been more embittered in some countries than in others is unclear.

Whatever the causes, some nations developed more centralized political systems than did others. Decision-making power may not have been shared in the latter systems, but at least veto groups able to limit royal power did arise. Interestingly, the growth of such checks to arbitrary power does not seem to have been related to the size of the territory governed. Despite the size of their domains, the Chinese emperors developed a highly centralized administrative structure, while the English kings, ruling a much smaller area, were unable to create an effective national bureaucracy and were frequently checked in their exercise of power by the aristocracy.

Countries which passed through the nation-building stage of their development before the twentieth century were not economically stagnant during this period. Commerce, both foreign and domestic, often flourished. While mainly agricultural, their economies also frequently involved a fair amount of manufacture. Industry was little mechanized, however, and the economy did not develop in the sense of experiencing a sustained, high rate of growth—the result of a fundamentally transformed productive process. For this process—industrialization—to be launched successfully, capital had to be concentrated to finance the equipment essential for volume production; people had to migrate from the country to the towns to provide a work force for industry; groups favorable to economic change had to gain a share in political power to eliminate the obstacles to growth; and economic decisions had to be made for economic reasons by those having the most accurate information.

During the nation-building stage the central government's need for money grew; it expanded its services and personnel and sought a world-power role. The more centralized the political system, the greater the need, for it had to support more elaborate structures. A monarch served by a reliable bureaucracy and a strong army did not have to bargain for financial support; he could extract it. Unfortunately for economic development, he was likely to extract it disproportionately from the new commercial class, thus thwarting the concentration of capital by the group most able to fulfill this function. The growing wealth of the commercial class was highly visible. Where political power was centralized, the class was unlikely to have anyone in a position to voice their interests effectively. Those holding power lacked commercial experience and did not understand the problems of or the conditions conducive to enterprise; they were likely to regard the economy as simply another source of power to be controlled to strengthen their political dominance. Thus economic decisions were politically, not economically, motivated. Such attitudes were also prevalent among the political elite in some decentralized systems, but there the national government lacked the power to implement them effectively.

An absence of rapport with governmental officials and a disproportionate tax burden was likely to create potentionally disruptive tensions by frustrating the commercial class. Since the government could not be certain that its efforts to assuage these tensions would succeed, it also had to attempt to prevent the commercial class's power from growing to the point where it could be a serious challenge. Permitting a relatively high level of social mobility was a good tactic for mollifying the *nouveau riche*. Since, in the centralized political system, the monarch dominated the aristocracy, he lost no power in permitting the commercial class to acquire prestige by buying its way into the aristocracy; he actually strengthened his position. Having arrived socially, the commercial class had satisfied its desire to be recognized and ceased to strive; its drive to achieve, to innovate, atrophied. In meeting the demands of the aristocratic style of life, it dissipated its wealth, instead of reinvesting it in further commercial development. To help insure that social mobility had these effects, some monarchs prohibited the aristocracy from commercial activity, as was done in France. The growth of a powerful commercial class was also checked in some countries by inheritance laws which divided estates among all the heirs instead of following the rule of primogeniture, another example of a policy which helped a centralized government avoid sharing its power and also hindered a development—capital concentration—requisite to beginning to industrialize.

The decentralized political system did not pose such a threat to private capital formation. Broadening existing institutions which limited royal power to include representatives of the commercial class did not seem as innovative as attempting to create such institutions where none had been established previously. The monarch's relative weakness meant that he could obtain the financial support he needed only if he granted the commercial class some means of expressing their interests. Furthermore, by allying with the commercial class he could strengthen his position against the aristocracy. Instead of dominating the commercial class, the monarch became dependent upon it. Even if he did not follow these policies, his ineffective bureaucracy prevented him from excessively burdening commercial wealth with heavy taxes hindering the growth of capital needed to begin industrialization.

The threat to capital concentration in decentralized political systems came not, then, from hostile government policy; the danger was excessive social mobility. If the commercial class could acquire both social prestige and political power, they might waste their wealth in aristocratic living rather than reinvest it in economic development. If the decentralized political system were not to have the same effect upon economic development as the centralized system, the *nouveau riche* had to remain social inferiors. This was the only instance, however, in which a closed society was essential. Upper mobility for the lower classes was an important means of strengthening the commercial class. The movement of aristocrats into commercial activity was equally important because it helped to convert them to middle-class values. Thus when the aristocracy and the commercial class eventually merged, democratic values—achievement instead of ascriptive values—predominated rather than elite values, as occurred when the two classes merged by the commercial class moving into the aristocracy.

The receptivity of the aristocracy to economic development and commercial values was affected significantly by their attitude toward agriculture. Where they regarded it as a business, where, as in England, they were directly involved in cultivating their lands and concerned, therefore, to discover more efficient and profitable, means of production, they had already acquired an outlook similar to the commercial class's prior to merging with them. Having embraced commercial values, they were able to move more easily into manufacturing enterprise and were less intransigent to industrial development than was an aristocracy like the French, whose world consisted of court life and intellectual pursuits rather than practical business affairs. The French aristocracy paid little attention to the management of their lands, preferring simply to collect a rent from the peasants, whom they allowed to work the land largely as though it were their own.

The French aristocracy's attitude hindered the development of an industrial economy not only because it made them unreceptive to economic change, but also because it meant they did little to impel the peasants to move into the towns where they would provide the labor force essential for industrialization. In England fewer agricultural laborers were required as the aristocracy moved from cultivating to the more profitable grazing. The English government assisted this change by passing the Enclosure Acts, which permitted the aristocracy to fence in the common land for pasture, thereby depriving the peasants of land they had used in the past. Thus the English aristocracy's commercial approach to agriculture severed the peasants' ties with the land and drove them from the rural areas.

In France, as in England, a peasant who wanted to move to town was not prevented from doing so, provided that he could save enough money to buy his freedom. The peasants' status was largely a matter of custom and reciprocal duties between them and the aristocracy, rather than a matter of law. Although the aristocracy in some countries was more directly interested in agriculture than the French aristocracy was, they did not develop the English commercial attitude. Instead of transforming the peasants into farm laborers, they tied them to the land as virtual hereditary serfs to avoid having to pay the level of wages which economic conditions demanded. This was especially the case in Russia, where the peasants were made serfs by government order. The escape route fairly common in Western Europe, of gaining freedom by living in a town for a specified period, was closed to the Russian peasant; he always remained a fugitive, subject to being returned to the land at any time. As a result Russia lacked the urban labor pool essential for industrial development. Although 10 to 15 percent of the population of Western Europe lived in towns during the medieval period, only two and a half percent of the Russians were town dwellers centuries later in 1630, and little more than four percent did not live in rural areas as late as 1796. What little manufacturing was done in Russia occurred on the aristocracy's estates and drew upon the serfs for manpower. Thus no urban commercial class arose in Russia, nor, of course, did a guild system develop—important checks upon arbitrary royal power in much of Western Europe.

Eliminating the peasants as a class not only aided economic development; it also reduced the possibilities of the political system becoming absolutistic. As long as a peasant class existed, so too did the possibility of a peasant revolution. Where the commercial class was especially weak, such a social upheaval was the only means of breaking the entrenched power of the landed aristocracy so that the economy could eventually be modernized. Thus in France the peasants were an important force in destroying the Ancien Regime. A more likely result in the twentieth century, however, was a Communist dictatorship, as occurred in China. The alternative danger was that the use of repressive measures to control the peasants would dispose a government to act similarly against the workers. Instead of being developed by private action, the economy would be modernized, after some delay, by the fiat of an illiberal, nationalistic regime. Germany and Italy furnish obvious examples of this progression.

To industrialize, a country needed a group that viewed the world in a new perspective, that desired to innovate. Since this process involved widespread, largely unforeseeable change, and therefore posed a threat to the status quo, the political authorities were not likely to initiate it. The impetus for change was more likely to come from a group having an independent economic base outside the political power structure, since advancing into a new stage of economic development required opening up the political system to remove or transform the structures that had impeded growth. This obviously could be achieved more easily in a decentralized system.

A centralized system retarded economic development even if the government was relatively receptive to economic innovation. With the economy directly under government control, only those who were permitted government posts could gain any experience in commercial activity. The negative effect of this was both qualitative and quantitative. Not only was the supply of those who had developed the commercial and managerial skills requisite to an industrial economy so restricted that rapid economic growth was impeded, but precisely those groups which historically have been best able to utilize this experience to contribute to economic development were foreclosed from it. Minority groups, for example, those who were not members of the established church in England, have provided to a very disproportionate extent the entrepreneurial abilities which now developed economies used when they began to industrialize. As outsiders—deviants from the basic norms or practices of their society—members of these groups were not likely to be recruited into government positions. Where the government ran the economy, they were also denied significant economic positions; the government unknowingly depriving itself of the talent it most needed to further economic growth.

The shift in political power to the commercial innovators was largely a shift in power from the aristocracy to the growing middle class—largely because, as previously noted, in some instances part of the aristocracy was commercially oriented and was not a major obstacle to economic change. Where this was true, the power shift was less violent than where the aristocracy's power had to be shattered by a peasant revolution before the political system could be opened up to economic change. Nonetheless, since even the aristocracy which was receptive to commercial values was more concerned with agriculture than manufacture, the shift in power was essential to insure that industrialization was not retarded. The middle class was able to expand its power relatively peacefully because the opportunity of quickly amassing huge, new fortunes lay in manufacture, not agriculture.

The rapid enrichment of some members of the middle class did not prevent a relatively slow, gradual transfer of power to the middle class as a class. When this was the pace of political change, the aristocracy was unlikely to view any single clash with the middle class as a fundamental threat to its position; it was asked to concede only a little power on each occasion. Thus, only when the aristocracy was no longer dominant did it realize how serious was the middle class's challenge to its power. The idea of perpetuating its power by allying, on its own terms, with the middle class did not occur to the aristocracy.

In some countries, however, such an alliance was the landed interests' strategy. Although still dominant, they were willing to join forces with the commercial interests because they recognized that the recent pace of industrialization meant that they could not avoid losing their position to the commercial class relatively soon; a pact seemed their only hope of salvaging some influence. The commercial class was less sanguine about its prospects because the growing strength and political awareness of the workers seemed a major threat. Thus it was anxious to obtain the aid of the landed interests in repressing the workers, who seemed to them the much more dangerous enemy. The German industrialists and agrarian Junkers, for example, allied in a politically illiberal, but at times paternalistic, regime toward the close of the nineteenth century. A similar development occurred in Italy in the twentieth century. After beginning to industrialize rapidly, the Italian economy was forced to retrench in adjusting to peacetime after the First World War. The resultant unemployment exacerbated working-class hostility toward the commercial class, making the latter desire the aid of the still-powerful landed interests. The repressive structures which the aristocracy had created to control the peasants were also directed against the workers, and the alliance culminated in a fascist regime.

A bifurcated agricultural interest helped the United States to develop differently. Increasingly toward the middle of the nineteenth century, Northern business interests cooperated with liberal Western agrarians rather than with the conservative, more elitist Southern agricultural oligarchy. This alliance did not produce the authoritarian threat to democracy which the coalition between business and agriculture did in Germany and Italy.

Where the commercial class was a junior partner of conservative landed interests, industrial development was not halted, since the commercial class shared in political power. The rate of development probably did not reach its optimum level, however, because the coalition bargain required respecting the interests of the landed group. Restricting the movement of peasants from farms to towns helped to insure that rural labor was so abundant that it could not demand effectively better working conditions. But the resultant shortage of urban workers threatened expanding industry with production bottlenecks.

Economic development was delayed even more where the commercial class was too weak to be even a junior partner. In Russia the peasants, assisted by a small, but strategically placed, working class, had to break the aristocrats' power before sustained industrial development could be implemented. In part because of the economy's relative backwardness (but also, of course, because of the Communist Party's ideology), the subsequent regime attempted to industrialize at a rapid pace, refused to share its power, and repressed all criticism. The cost of industrialization in human terms in the form of forced labor and execution of opponents like the kulaks was enormous.

The workers did not fare much better in liberal, democratic systems, where the commercial class gradually won sufficient power from the landed groups to become dominant. When this occurred in Britain and the United States at different times during the nineteenth century, the workers were not yet well-organized. The commercial class usually did not have to invoke the government's power to repress the workers; it simply desired the government to remain aloof so that it had a free hand to treat the workers as it pleased to extract from them the costs of industrialization. The best to be said of such a system, which certainly produced its share of human misery, is that at least a tradition of coercive government was not established—unlike the alliance between an apprehensive commercial class and a conservative landed interest to repress the workers and the peasants. Thus, as the working class grew and organized, the potential of broadening the system into a mass democracy was greater.

To summarize: First, for an agricultural, limited production economy to begin sustained industrialization, the political system must be sufficiently decentralized (or ineffective, if centralized) so that the central government cannot hinder the private amassing of capital. A democratic political system is more likely to develop eventually in a system in which power is dispersed rather than concentrated. Secondly, industrial development requires a major expansion of the urban labor force, which can occur only if the peasants are transformed into workers. This process is facilitated if the landed aristocracy views agriculture as a commercial enterprise. When the peasants are transformed and not repressed, a tradition of coercive government is not established and the chances of subsequent modernization being carried out by either a right-wing or a left-wing autocratic regime are reduced greatly.

The third essential for industrial growth is a shift in political power to the commercial innovators, so that the landed aristocracy will be unable to halt development to guard its interests from injury. By winning power gradually, the commercial class creates a precedent for subsequent piecemeal broadening of the political system to include representatives of the workers.

Finally, the beginnings of successful industrial development require those who have the most accurate information to make economic decisions for economic reasons. This is most likely to be the case if a political system is decentralized sufficiently during the nation-building stage so that the central government is unable to direct the economy effectively. The economy is industrialized, then, largely independently of the government; when this occurs, new power centers develop, which not only press for expanded political rights but also have sufficient economic strength so that their demands cannot be ignored.

Thus the decentralized, limited political system most conducive to initiating industrial development is also the system having the greatest potential for eventually evolving into a democracy. This is not to say that a decentralized system which has no peasant class, and in which the commercial class gradually triumphs over the landed aristocracy, must develop into a democracy; subsequent events will obviously affect its development. Such a system is simply a propitious start toward democracy. The fact that it also facilitates launching an industrial economy helps make more understandable the association between democracy and economic development in the middle of the twentieth century.

As this summary indicates, industrialization is best initiated privately for both political and economic reasons; the government's economic role at this stage of development should be limited. As industrialization proceeds, however, government can aid development by participating more actively in the economy. In countries which successfully developed industrial economies a half century or more ago, the government encouraged the growth of banking and credit systems and maintained a stable currency to help make capital more readily available for industrial investment. An improved communications network had to be constructed, for economic units were no longer as autonomous as they had been during the nation-building period. To be properly integrated, this network had to be centrally coordinated to some extent. Some governments invested directly in projects facilitating communications, while others attempted to allocate private resources for this purpose through inducements like tax benefits or grants of free land to private companies willing to build railroads, as was done in the United States. Rapid growth of the capital goods industries was essential; a common means of achieving this growth was protective tariffs.

Although at this stage government assistance was beneficial in mobilizing and allocating resources, management remained largely in private hands. The economy had become more integrated, but its units were still sufficiently autonomous so that the problems of central economic direction noted during the nation-building period continued to exist. Only in very few instances, in which one sector of an economy had become integrated much more tightly than the economy as a whole, could the government beneficially manage resources directly if it were not to hinder industrial development.

The government's role in socializing and integrating society also expanded. Educational opportunities had to be greatly enlarged to provide adequate numbers of people with the technical skills essential to operating an industrial economy. Associated with this was a shift toward selecting people for governmental and private positions of responsibility on the basis of ability rather than family connection or social status—recruitment by competence rather than ascription. At the same time, however, those who succeeded in commerce were hailed as the most able members of society and were recognized as having talents which fitted them for almost any important activity. By bestowing such prestige on the commercial class, society helped to steer those with great drive and inventiveness toward industry so that their abilities could be used to expand the economy rapidly.

Education also was a means of inculcating values and thus controlling behavior. Performance of this function was especially important because migration from the sparsely populated countryside to congested urban areas introduced many people to environments and styles of living vastly different from those with which they had been familiar. Behavior which had been proper was now irrelevant, old value systems crumbled, and life sometimes seemed filled with threats and tensions. Government could do little to improve the lower classes' living and working conditions which would not slow economic growth; both welfare programs, which would have required increased taxes on the wealthy, and more humane labor standards, which almost certainly would have raised production costs, would have restricted the rewards of enterprise and reduced the amount of capital available for investment in industrial development. The workers had to bear the cost of sustained industrialization.

In such circumstances, social tensions were understandably more prevalent. The government's role in enforcing social values expanded, therefore; fulfillment of this function could not be left to custom and private groups, as had been largely the practice during the nation-building stage, for most of the groups capable of playing this role had been destroyed in the mass shift of people to the urban areas.

If governments were to perform these several new functions successfully, they had to be more centralized, had to develop a more effective bureaucracy. The type of political system which developed depended significantly upon the traditions established during the nation-building and early industrial periods. Once initiated, industrialization has been developed further under democratic, communistic, and fascistic or elitist regimes. Of these three, the pace of development was fastest in the communistic, since the shift of power to those striving to develop the economy was gradual in the democratic systems, and concessions by the commercial class to agricultural interests thwarted a maximum rate of development under the fascistic or elitist system. Whether, then, the typical pattern for political conflict was riot followed by repression or petition followed by limited concession, whether the system was coercive or competitive, bargaining obviously made a tremendous difference, since economic development did not necessitate a particular type of political system. I have already discussed the crucial variables conducive to the development of one type of system or another. The basic point is that while the costs and burdens of industrial development always fell most heavily upon the lower classes, the prospects of gradually developing a democratic political system were greater if repressive controls over labor were kept to a minimum and usually imposed by private power centers rather than by the government.

The development of the United States at the close of the nineteenth century and the beginning of the twentieth illustrates this point quite well. In most industrializing countries the basic political problem was to insure that political power was not conceded to the working class so rapidly that they were able to divert scarce capital away from investment for industrial expansion into improvement of living conditions. In contrast, the United States was a mass democracy before it began industrializing at a sustained rate. The problem, then, was not the European one of limiting concessions; rather, it was the problem of checking the already empowered democratic forces so that they would not hinder economic devlopment.

Fortunately, these forces did not have to be constrained to the extent of killing an already flourishing democracy. Social mobility was high and, compared to Europe, society was little stratified, thus encouraging the idea that one had only to work hard to get ahead rapidly. Fortunes were still being made in the West and even workers who did not migrate could regard themselves as potential small businessmen. Working-class solidarity was weakened further by the ethnic diversity of labor, which hindered cooperation even among those of similar occupational status. To many of the recent immigrants, who made up a significant proportion of the labor force, living conditions that were bad by American standards were considerably better than what they had left in Europe; thus they had little reason to be discontented. As a result of such factors, labor was not very strong in the United States and posed no real threat to the concentration of capital for investment. In most cases employers were able to repress the working class adequately without invoking the government's power. Thus official coercive machinery which subsequently might have jeopardized the growth of democracy was little developed.

This example also helps to illuminate a significant point concerning the essential shift in power from the traditional elite to the commercial innovators. The commercial class needed to control the government, but not in order to impose economic modernization through government command, for such a system would be highly likely to develop into a fascist regime. Rather, the commercial class needed control to eliminate the obstacles thwarting or likely to thwart economic development. The government in systems that evolved into democracies did not so much develop the economy as assist the efforts of those who wished to do this for personal gain, and allowed them a relatively free hand in their efforts, intervening only on those few occasions when private power proved insufficient to achieve a particular goal.

When the government, rather than private groups, modernized the economy, potential alternative power centers did not grow out of the process of economic change. In the Soviet Union, for example, the economic modernizers used governmental power not only to repress the workers, but also to direct them in implementing official plans for economic development. All worker organizations were government-sponsored. Virtually no nongovernmental economic groups were permitted to exist. Thus interests that balanced governmental power and were able to press effectively for expanded political rights in some countries were unable to affect the Soviet Union's political development significantly.

Upon achieving self-sustaining growth, an industrial economy could increasingly allocate capital for welfare purposes; once the water has begun to flow, the pump no longer needs to be primed. Instead of insuring that a limited supply of investment capital was not dissipated in alleviating squalor marginally, the government began to help ameliorate the workers' life. In constitutional, limited government systems this was accomplished in part by initiating social welfare programs and imposing standards of labor conditions, and in part by extending a share in political power to the workers through measures such as broadening the franchise. These concessions gave the workers a growing stake in society and made them see reform as a more effective strategy than revolution.

To a lesser extent, similar trends characterize industrial communistic countries hoping to develop into diversified, technologically sophisticated, abundant economies. Detailed, autocratic management by the government can bring an economy from early to self-sustaining industrialization. However, to realize an economic system's potential sufficiently to achieve abundance, appears to require some relaxation of control. A worker who does not benefit from economic growth can be coerced to put in his time, but probably will not devote to his task the effort he would if his labor were voluntary. Inventiveness is rarely encouraged by ukase. Even relatively unskilled labor can produce better results when it is not coerced, as the Soviet Union has learned in agriculture. Peasants on collective farms are permitted to cultivate their small garden plots only after they have worked the requisite time on the collective lands. Yet these plots, which total less than one and a half percent of all the Soviet Union's agricultural land, yield over half of all the milk and meat and most of the eggs produced in the Soviet Union.

Detailed, central economic management of a modern economy is also likely to be inefficient because the economy is so complex and interrelated that even vastly improved communications and data processing systems cannot provide all the information necessary for rational decision making in a completely planned economy. Some decentralization is essential for the economy of abundance, as the Soviet Union's experiments with increased factory autonomy and profits suggest it has come to recognize.

These comments do not imply that the Soviet Union must become, or is likely to become, a democracy before the end of the twentieth century. The point is that the Soviet Union can advance more successfully into abundance by decentralizing its economy and that such decentralization, especially given the close interrelation of politics and economics in the Soviet Union, also involves some political decentralization. Further economic development will probably mean, then, that the Soviet Union will not be as dictatorial a system as it has been in the past, even though it does not evolve into a constitutional democracy.

Examining the experience of most industrialized nations, then, helps to establish that the relation discovered between degree of democracy and level of economic development is not merely happenstance. The political system most conducive to starting industrialization also has the greatest potential of developing into a democracy. That democracy and development do not correlate perfectly can be explained, however, by the fact that subsequent industrialization can be carried out with almost equal facility by a highly or moderately centralized system, by a dictatorial or constitutional regime. Once a system achieves self-sustaining economic growth, it is able to generate a sufficient supply of capital so that extending political power to the lower economic classes no longer threatens industrialization. Furthermore, if a system is to realize fully its economic potential, to achieve affluence, it must not be so highly centralized that it causes a complex, highly integrated modern economy to operate at less than maximum efficiency. Thus, economic conditions argue for a lessening of repressive measures in dictatorial regimes with advanced industrial economies.

These arguments may not be compelling; dictatorial leaders are hardly likely to abandon readily the procedures and values with which they are familiar to embrace a constitutionalism which seems foreign to them. Economic growth is not a philosopher's stone able to transmute dictatorship into democracy. However, the pressures of advanced development do encourage some decentralizing and, to that extent, some moderating of totalitarianism.

The routes a system may travel from a traditional to an affluent economy are varied; the stages through which it may pass are several. Some stages and routes are more conducive than others to constitutional government; even these, however, cannot compel a system to transform itself into a democracy. But while the relation between democracy and economic development is not necessary, neither is it accidental. As the preceding survey of political and economic development in industrially advanced nations shows, these two factors are not insulated from each other. There are good reasons why we should find that they are interrelated in the middle of the twentieth century.

The Impact of Development in New Nations

Despite the significance of the discovery of these historical patterns of relations between political and economic development, they will remain merely ways of understanding past events unless they can be shown to be relevant to the experience of the many countries now attempting to evolve from traditional to more developed systems. Can these patterns be applied to new nations? Will they permit us to anticipate accurately the likely course of events?

Unfortunately, little comparative research has been carried out on this topic thus far. Conclusions and beliefs on the subject rely even more heavily upon logic and informed speculation than they do on the topic just discussed. Various studies have helped, however, to clarify the extent to which contemporary developing nations must cope with conditions which differ from those that faced countries now economically advanced when they were at a similar stage in their development.

Economic development appears to offer an opportunity to democratize a political system. An advanced economy provides a base for associational groups, which, as pointed out in the last chapter, contribute significantly to a democratic political culture. By disrupting old norms and procedures, economic modernization makes possible the implanting of participant values in place of the more passive conceptions of the individual political role typical of traditional societies. In contemporary developing countries, however, economic change is more likely to generate antidemocratic trends.

In the second half of the twentieth century the chances are slight of a country successfully beginning to industrialize spontaneously with its government's economic role restricted. Technological advances have made the development of resources, even when these are plentiful, and the building of an industrial economy, considerably more costly than they were in the nineteenth century. A developing country must employ the most efficient, up-to-date techniques, despite their expense, in order to compete effectively with more modern systems. Private interests, even if unburdened by the government, are usually unable to amass sufficient capital to launch industrialization.

The rapid growth of population characteristic of developing nations means that they must divert a considerable portion of their wealth from investment to consumption simply to prevent mass starvation. The shortage of capital is so acute that the government can permit little haphazard expenditure, if it is to have any prospect of developing the economy. Even when the government mobilizes capital for development investment, the supply will probably be inadequate. Therefore, the government will need to seek foreign aid to supplement domestic capital; administering this aid will also involve it directly in the economy. The government can hardly avoid responsibility for economic development. The political impact of government assuming such responsibility, however, is to lower the chances that alternate power centers able to limit the government's power effectively will arise.

Another major reason why political power is not likely to be dispersed widely in contemporary developing countries is that the stages of development are telescoped. In contrast to the pattern followed by most Western, industrialized countries, the new nations are seeking to launch industrialization before they have firmly established their political systems, and thus they are also burdened with the task of building a nation—creating a sense of national identity. For the government to permit other power centers to exist or even to tolerate formal opposition or dissent, is to risk the rupture of the fragile bounds holding the country together. Economic modernization's disruptive impact on traditional ways of life is more likely to be a threat to, instead of an opportunity for, democratic development.[2] In a society where familiar norms and procedures are crumbling, rapid industrialization and urbanization can easily destroy, rather than transform, intermediate groups and political structures. The resultant break in continuity jeopardizes political legitimacy and, therefore, political stability.

This danger is aggravated because so many people in contemporary developing countries are dissatisfied. Unlike the populace in nations which industrialized in the nineteenth century, their appetites have been whetted by the achievements of the prosperous nations. Yet their demands must be resisted to provide capital for development. The conflict is further exacerbated because a safety valve which helped to reduce the explosive pressures of industrialization for European nations now operates only to a limited extent. In the past malcontents might migrate to Canada, Australia, or the United States; now, little discontent can be drained off in this way. Immigration is much more restricted, especially for racial groups from developing countries.

A government attempting both to build a nation and to achieve in a decade or two the level of economic development which other nations attained over perhaps a century is unlikely to compromise its policies to accommodate dissenting views or to be greatly concerned with protecting individual liberties.[3] Rather, its primary goal must be to maintain itself. The instruments of violence, which even a government that can afford only outdated American military equipment possess to defend itself, are considerably more overpowering than those available a century ago. The abortive Hungarian Revolution of 1956 reemphasized the obvious fact that rocks are no match for tanks. Governments clearly are stronger now in relation to their people than they were when Western nations began to industrialize. But the ability to coerce support is not unlimited. Thus perhaps an even more significant strengthening of government is the enhancing of its ability to control public opinion.

Mass communications channels permeate many developing

countries much more thoroughly than they did now-industrialized countries when they were beginning to develop their economies. The possibilities for propagandizing even a largely illiterate society are immensely greater now than in the past. Such efforts are especially likely to be effective in countries rapidly developing their economies, since, as already noted, this process tends to destroy intermediate groups. The absence of intervening structures insulating the people from leaders' efforts to manipulate them promotes a politics of antidemocratic mass movements. Political parties and electoral systems appear at an earlier historical stage than they did in countries which are now industrialized. Not having developed out of an increased political awareness or as concessions to demands for more equal political power, these political structures are likely to be noncompetitive. Instead of functioning as they have in Western democratic systems to call the government to account, they are used by the government to politicize and control the population. Thus, broadening the opportunities for political participation does not necessarily make a system more democratic.

A rapid increase in participation may in fact hinder the development of democracy by threatening the stability of a system which does not possess institutionalized political structures to channel, perhaps even to restrict, participation.[4] Institutionalized political structures are adaptable to new functions and personnel, complex in organization and diversified in purpose, well-integrated and disciplined internally, and autonomous—having established values and procedures of their own. Institutionalized parties, for example, are founded on member adherence to a set of policy alternatives or to a general orientation to politics, rather than on personal loyalty to a leader. In the institutionized political system, associational interest groups are at least as common and influential as institutional and nonassociational groups and are capable of laboring for new causes as some of their original goals are achieved. The strength of a political system with institutionalized structures is that it is able to bear the weight of widespread participation without collapsing into the virtual anarchy of poorly established systems where power, procedures, leaders, and structures are all ephemeral.

Institutionalizing political structures obviously requires time. To endure, then, a contemporary developing country may have to buy time by restricting political participation until institutionalization catches up. This may require disagreeable policies such as expanding educational opportunity at a lower rate than possible in order to avoid demands from a more literate populace for a greater role in the making of authoritative decisions. Unfortunately, this step may also slow the rate of economic development. A competitive party system may be more of a debit than an asset in a society whose political structures are little institutionalized. Where political traditions are few and national consciousness poorly developed, sharply competing parties are liable to produce a fragmented, rather than a consensual, political culture.

Thus far scholars have done little more than speculate about which means are most effective for achieving a consensual political culture in a new nation. Huntington has suggested that a political party may be the most valuable instrument for fostering national unity. A party provides an outlet for the burgeoning desire to participate in politics, yet also can serve as a means of controlling this desire so that it does not overburden and destroy fragile political structures. Thus, a party helps provide the time needed to institutionalize these structures. Furthermore, when the party's goals are not challenged by competitors, they can serve as the foundation for a widely accepted value system.

Yet, as previously noted, if intermediate structures are nonexistent, a single party can be an instrument of manipulating public opinion, thus making any popular participation in politics virtually meaningless. An institutionalized single party as much concerned to propagate norms as to devise policy alternatives to public problems is at least as likely to generate a coercive political culture as a consensual culture. Instead of moderating the impact of mass participation, it may throttle it; instead of blending the participant role with the subject and apolitical roles to produce the citizen who can function through structures that have had time to institutionalize themselves, such a party may arrest individual political development at the subject stage.

As an alternate means of uniting the people of a developing country and encouraging their adherence to the political system, Almond and Verba stress a symbolic event or a charismatic leader. The French Revolution and the Paris Commune of 1870, while certainly symbolic events, alienated Frenchmen from each other, however, rather than welding them together. And in another study, Almond himself has pointed out the charismatic leader's potential threat to democracy.[5] Such a leader may seek to unify a fragmented political culture synthetically through a coercive nationalistic movement. Not only do individual liberties suffer in such a totalitarian regime, but the problem of lack of national unity is really not solved. Behind the facade of charismatic nationalism the old conflicts still fester, ready to break forth again when the movement collapses with the passing of the leader from the country's political life.

Every charismatic leader does not create a totalitarian regime, of course, as Charles de Gaulle has shown in France. De Gaulle illustrates the point that the charismatic leader's ability to unify a nation is limited, for although he is the quintessential charismatic leader, he has sharply divided, rather than united, Frenchmen. Furthermore, few people expect his structural reforms to survive long after he leaves French politics. This, Huntington argues, is the failing of charismatic leaders: they are loathe to institutionalize their system of rule, since establishing regular procedures and delegating responsibility to other structures would restrict their own powers. Thus at best they contribute little to political development; at worst they foster an antidemocratic political system.

While, then, in the past industralization was most likely to be launched successfully in systems which had the greatest potential of developing into democracies, this is not very likely to remain true in the new nations. Considerable government involvement in developing the economy is much more probable, much more essential than formerly. Governments now have available much more effective means of controlling and manipulating the population. The prospects for democracy cannot be bright in a system of centralized and pervasive government.

Extraconstitutional Change

While, as is clear from the preceding discussion, economic development so disrupts political and social structures that it is difficult to consider it peaceful change, this process can be distinguished from extraconstitutional change, although it may help to produce such change. Political change which does not conform with constitutional norms and procedures is not unusual; in fact, it is more common than change which does conform. Thus a study of political development which considered only evolutionary, constitutional change—however significant its impact—would be incomplete.

A major obstacle to the study of extraconstitutional change is the lack of any generally accepted scheme for classifying various types of such change. Riot, rebellion, revolution, coup, and insurrection are some of the terms used to refer to behavior associated with extraconstitutional change. Such terms have been defined so imprecisely and in so many different ways, however, that distinguishing between them in the abstract is frequently impossible, to say nothing of attempting to decide which label applies to actual instances of extraconstitutional change. This is not a trivial what's-in-a-name problem; when definitions are so vague or idiosyncratic that one researcher includes in his study cases which another excludes, the search for patterns of political change is thwarted, since their findings are obviously not comparable. In such circumstances, one study can neither refute nor confirm another; they are simply irrelevant to each other.

In view of the rudimentary state of research on extraconstitutional change, I will distinguish only grossly between coups and revolutions. A revolution is an extraconstitutional transfer of political power to a segment of society different from that formerly holding power; it transforms society by creating new social and political structures. A coup is an extraconstitutional transfer of control of governmental organs to another faction of the dominant elite which hardly alters the social and political systems. Revolution is obviously a more fundamental change and is more likely to involve mass participation.

According to these definitions, although violent, extraconstitutional change is common in Latin American countries, revolutions are few.[6] Despite extraconstitutional changes of those occupying the top political posts, the social hierarchy is typically unaltered, control of the economy remains in the same hands, and even the government's policy continues basically unchanged. In these systems, where many of the routes to economic advancement are closed to some groups, control of the government serves as an alternative means of enrichment. The typical political leader seeks not to destroy the established bases of social and economic power, but only to direct a sizable share of government funds to his family and friends and to capitalize on confidential information. Since these goals do not fundamentally threaten the social and economic elite, extraconstitutional change can be relatively bloodless—limited both in duration and in number of participants.

When the aim of extraconstitutional change is to transform society, however, much more is at stake and the conflict is likely to be considerably more contentious.[7] The economically depressed, stagnant society is not likely to spawn attempts to secure such fundamental change. People in such societies are so downtrodden that they become resigned to despair. Withdrawn into themselves, they lack the community feeling essential for the joint action that launches a revolutionary movement. The post-World War II colonial independence movements, which, given their transfer of power from a foreign to a domestic elite and their subsequent transformation of society, must be considered revolutions, are a major exception to this point, since they did occur in economically impoverished societies. In these cases nationalistic fervor directed against an obviously foreign ruling elite generated feelings of solidarity among even the poverty-stricken and provided them with a goal which the military reverses their colonial rulers had suffered during the war suggested was realizable.

Revolution against a domestic rather than a foreign elite is more likely, however, in a society that is progressing economically. Improving conditions arouse hopes of satisfying ever-expanding desires. (In the newer nations these hopes may derive more from expanding knowledge of economically developed nations, rather than from any domestic progress.) Should progress halt, these hopes of self-improvement are frustrated and an intolerable gap between expected and actual satisfactions develops.[8] Class conflict is sharpest not between the rich and the poor, but between the traditional, aristocratic elite and those whose economic success is recent and as yet unmatched with the enhanced social status and increased political power which they feel their demonstrated abilities merit. If they believe that the check to their hopes of further advancement is due to the government's unknowledgeable limits on enterprise, they will not only feel cramped, but will also begin to fear that their past gains are in jeopardy.

As long as the government does not appear to thwart the development of one's potential, a person is not as likely to feel threatened by the political system, even if many of his desires for advancement are frustrated. Directing discontent against either the political or the economic elites in the United States during the Depression, for example, was difficult, since by 1933 the government appeared to be doing its best to alleviate conditions and business was cooperating with it. Popular values and the political culture were also significant factors in preventing the growth of revolutionary sentiment. Many Americans continued to believe that eventual success was certain and could be achieved by hard work. They were convinced also that change should occur within the existing political framework, since it was fundamentally sound.

Economically developing societies are susceptible to revolutionary change not only because they may falter in fulfilling their promise of a better life, but also because the traditional means of regulating social strains are likely to be enervated in such societies. Mass movement to the cities and growth of industries enfeebles traditional norms and the traditional elite, rendering them relatively useless in checking protest. This development is especially inimical to stability, since protest tends to be prevalent in economically developing societies. Technological change jeopardizes the status and wealth of some groups and burdens many with adapting to new procedures—the regimenting of their time by factory work rules, for example. The substantial costs of development fall more heavily on some groups than on others, thus causing discontent.

Unlike the societies in which they operated, the governments overthrown by revolutions were not financially sound. Too unadaptable to cope with the new problems caused by economic advance, they were too inefficient even to finance their own operations. This failure was symptomatic of their ineffectiveness in other spheres, especially in maintaining order and monopolizing force. They were increasingly unable to control illegal challenges to their authority. In some instances defeat in a foreign war so weakened the military forces that they could not combat a domestic crisis effectively; in other cases these forces' loyalty was compromised because they questioned the government's legitimacy. When, for example, the Czar's troops, contrary to their behavior in 1905, refused to obey their orders to fire on the mobs in the streets in 1917, the Czar's rule was obviously at an end. Such legitimacy crises are not confined to military forces; even some of the ruling elite may begin to question whether their group is entitled to control political power. Such doubts lessen their willingness to employ violence against even revolutionary opponents.

Thus the government disintegrates and, unlike a coup, the revolutionaries do not so much seize power as fill a power vacuum. Furthermore, in a coup the new authority develops within the old, while in a revolution it is external to the old. The revolutionaries seek to stir up mass disobedience to destroy the existing order so that they can replace it with a new one; those who plan a coup wish to control the masses through the existing order and simply desire the masses to acquiesce in a shift of control over the power structure from one faction of the dominant elite to another.

Although well-organized revolutionary movements play an important part in stimulating and directing discontent against the existing system and in guiding the popular uprising when it erupts, the revolution does not proceed in conformity with a single master plan. As the old order crumbles, popularly based structures—soviets, communes—arise spontaneously to perform the functions which the government no longer performs, and to involve the citizens more directly in public affairs than the old restrictive power structure would permit. Thus in creating a new order the revolutionaries either must make their well-organized movement the government, and eliminate all other political structures, or join the popularly based structures so that they can control them in their performance of governmental functions.

Limited evidence on the pattern of behavior after destruction of the old order suggests that the group initially in authority is either more moderate than some of its fellow revolutionaries or becomes so as it begins to deal with the responsibilities of authoritative decision making. The rule of the moderates fails to satisfy the extremists, who begin to oppose their former colleagues. The moderates fail to restrict the extremists' growing power, since to do so would make the moderates feel that they were no different from the old elite who had oppressed them. Eventually the extremists are able to seize power in a coup. Their rule rapidly develops into a reign of terror—the government proclaims the only truth, which everyone must accept completely; it seeks to regulate even the most trivial details of everyday life; it purges all who are even suspected of being opponents.

Eventually this fervor dies out. The government continues to utter an ideology but this is more ritual than belief. Although less totalitarian, the government remains dictatorial. It is more centralized and effective than the regime it replaced. This by no means implies, however, that the average person is any better off than he was under the old regime. In fact, since the revolution so dislocates society that economic conditions deteriorate drastically, particularly during the reign of terror, most people require considerable time simply to regain their former economic level. As for their political circumstances, the old regime's increasing ineffectiveness greatly restricted its ability to tyrannize them, while the new regime's centralized power is virtually unchecked.

It is so obvious as to be jejune that government can avoid a revolution by fulfilling the rising expectations of its people. Since this often will be impossible, especially in overpopulated, resource-poor, economically undeveloped nations, the alternative may be to clamp down forcibly on expectations to keep them from outstripping the government's capacity to deliver. Implementing this course requires strong and loyal police and military forces. But foreign affairs largely outside a government's control, such as defeat in a war, may prevent it from maintaining such forces.

However, as my previous comment on the United States and its Depression indicated, popular adherence to a regime is not always based simply on whether people are satisfied with the government's output. If a political system is to endure through good times and bad without having to trust in force, most of its citizens must consider it legitimate. Legitimacy helps to compensate for ineffective or distasteful policies; a man who believes that the political system is legitimate does not revolt even though he opposes the government's policies.

Lipset argues that if democratizing a political system alienates conservative groups, the system will be unstable since such groups will consider it illegitimate.[9] Because most of the English-speaking and West European stable democracies are monarchies, he concludes that the best way to avoid alienating conservative groups is to retain the monarch as a magnet for traditional loyalties while broadening a society's power base.[10]

Regardless of whether Lipset's analysis is valid, his conclusion hardly seems applicable to the world's new nations. Smacking of imperialism, monarchy holds little attraction for recently independent nations. Except for the "Old Dominions"—Canada, New Zealand, and Australia—few members of the British Commonwealth remained monarchies once they were fully independent and could become republics, if they so desired. Nor does an indigenous monarchy seem a suitable alternative for such systems. Unless a country were to inaugurate a ruling house, which would be of little use in attracting loyalties initially since it would have little continuity with the past, it would have to seek a monarch among tribal leaders, who are hardly likely to be modernizers. Such a monarch could only be an obstacle to the rapid pace of development desired in an economically undeveloped country.

A feeling of political competence—the belief that one can participate effectively in the process of making authoritative decisions—may encourage a person to consider legitimate the political system under which he lives, according to Almond and Verba's research.[11] In Mexico an aspiring democracy, even though feelings of political competency do not make people more satisfied with the government's action, they still increase popular attachment to the system itself. In the stable democracies of Britain and the United States, those who believe they can participate effectively are both more satisfied with the government's output and with the system itself than are those who do not feel competent. In either case opportunities to participate help to win legitimacy for the system.

The chance to participate wins support also in the unstable democracies of Italy and Germany, but on a more pragmatic basis. In those countries, people who believe they can participate effectively are more likely to be satisfied with the government's specific output and are loyal to the system for this reason. Since their feelings of political competency do not increase their adherence to the system as such, however, their support is less resolute than is true of political competents in the other two types of systems.

Nonetheless, by one means or another, democracy, by broadening the opportunities for people to participate in the decision-making process, increases its support and helps to avoid revolutionary discontent. Yet participation is not a panacea. A political system whose structures are not institutionalized—which is quite likely to be the case in transitional systems—can collapse, as Huntington warns, under the pressure of too widespread participation. Thus, institutionalizing political structures and creating legitimacy are Herculean tasks. Where they are not accomplished, however, extraconstitutional change is likely. For it is difficult to believe that economic development will encounter no obstacles and, as we have seen, when economic progress halts or fails to satisfy the hopes and desires which it has stimulated, a potential revolutionary situation occurs. Lacking a fund of legitimacy to allay discontent, the government can resort only to force to repress opposition. Whether it succeeds in controlling its opponents or falls to their challenge, the resultant political process is likely to be even less democratic than its predecessor. Thus economic development can be inimical to democratic development.

While the impact of economic development upon democracy and political stability is especially a problem for traditional and transitional political systems, modern systems can also be affected significantly by economic factors. Even without exploring this complex problem in detail, it is clear that one of the factors which led to the collapse of the Weimar Republic and the Nazi triumph in Germany in 1933 was the inability of the government to deal with the economic problems the country encountered in the 1920s and 1930s. The case illustrates well the crucial role of legitimacy. The Germans were not only dissatisfied with the performance of their government, but were little committed to it; many of them felt that the politicians had betrayed the army by agreeing to an armistice when the war had not been lost and then signing an excessively harsh peace treaty. Thus, when a crisis of effectiveness occurred, the government could not rely upon feelings of legitimacy to see it through until better economic times. Economic expectations were not fulfilled, the political system was not valued, and the government was unable to utilize force effectively to deal with challenges to its authority. The result was not a revolution in the sense of a group using force to gain control of the government—Hitler attained the Chancellorship by legal means. The system which the Nazis quickly implemented, however, varied so drastically from the Weimar Republic as to make labeling this change a revolution not inappropriate.

Although, then, as the early part of this chapter explained, there are good reasons why democracy and a high level of economic development should be associated, the latter by no means insures the former and the process of attaining a highly developed economy is not, in the middle of the twentieth century, congenial to the development of a democratic political system or to the avoidance of extraconstitutional change.

Chapter 4

Expressing and Focusing Demands
for Authoritative Decisions

In the United States, about two-thirds of the adult population votes in a Presidential election. During the last twenty-five years, at least three-fourths, and usually more, of eligible British voters have participated in elections for the House of Commons, while in New Zealand the turnout for elections is about 90 percent and in Australia even higher. I cite these figures not to prove that democracy is more vigorous in one country than another—the figures are not really comparable, since voting is compulsory in Australia and lack of the figure for the total national electorate in the United States forces calculating participation on the basis of the number of people over 21, many of whom are not registered or are otherwise disqualified—but to indicate that my argument in the first chapter, that control of the government is so valuable a prize that everyone should be interested in politics, is not universally accepted. Many people—perhaps 25,000,-000 in the United States—do not exercise their power to help select the single most important governmental official; they do not express their interests to the government.

You might think that these nonvoters are people who require no assistance and that people most likely to make demands on the government are most in need of help or protection. Yet such people, minors and the uneducated, for example, are least likely to know how to express their needs effectively and are more likely to be resigned to their circumstances because they have lost hope for improving their lives. Those who are most defenseless are precisely the people who may hesitate to express their needs because they cannot protect themselves from reprisal for daring to question their lot.

To understand who governs requires studying who does participate in politics, who does express demands on the government. What structures are available to assist them in obtaining the action they desire from the government? To what extent do these structures alter demands and how do they affect the political process?

Class and Political Activity

Understandably, the level of political interest and activity varies considerably from one country to another. Most people in the United States, Britain, and Germany feel that the government's action is relevant to their lives and, therefore, follow political affairs, while half or more of the population in Italy and Mexico feel that the government is irrelevant to them personally and are uninterested in politics.[1]

Despite such national differences, however, many characteristics of political participants are the same in many countries.[2] Those who are least likely to vote or to be active politically in other ways are those whose income or education is low, those who are under 35, unmarried, or belong to few, if any, organizations, or unskilled workers, marginal farmers, or women. Although such people participate little through the normal political structures, some of them are likely to be active in antidemocratic mass movements. Mass movements draw support primarily from those with few social ties, particularly marginal farmers and businessmen, the unemployed, and students. Those who participate most in "constitutional" politics possess characteristics opposite from those of the low participators, except that political activity tends to decline after a person reaches 60.

Other findings about those who participate in politics help to explain why high social and economic status and education should be associated with high political activity. The better educated are more likely to be informed on public affairs. The information acquired by those with high status is more likely to have some political content; the people with whom they talk are more likely to discuss politics. Thus these people are more likely than others to receive political stimuli and those receiving more such stimuli are most likely to be active. More highly educated people with higher status are more likely to feel obligated to participate in politics and people who feel obligated to participate are more likely actually to participate. People who feel they can affect the government's actions are more likely to participate in politics than those who feel they cannot, and better educated men with higher status occupations are most likely to believe they can affect the government. Finally, while those who are cynical about politics or alienated from the political system are less likely to participate than those who have a more positive image, people whose status and education are high are less likely to be cynical or alienated; thus, their rate of participation is not reduced by feelings of cynicism.

Whether a person is active in a political party seems to be linked with somewhat different characteristics.[3] This is not especially surprising, since it is possible for a person to follow politics without being attached to a party. In both the United States and Norway the proportion of people who identify with a political party is affected little by sex or level of education. Less well educated men do tend somewhat, however, to be strong identifiers, and highly educated men to be independents. As for occupation, white-collar workers tend slightly to be independents and farmers to be strong identifiers. The older a person is, the more likely he is to adhere to a party.

Fathers' partisan preferences significantly affect their childrens', but the impact of this factor varies from one country to another.[4]

People in both France and the United States who know what party their fathers prefer usually identify with a party themselves, while those who do not know are as likely not to favor any party as to feel a tie with one. Few French fathers, however, communicate their preferences to their children either explicitly or implicitly. As a result, considerably fewer people in France than in the United States identify with a political party even though the impact of family politicization is as strong in one country as another.

The nature of a country's parties affects whether those who identify with a party become active in it. High education and occupational status are not so important in recruiting active members if parties are rather homogeneous, class-oriented groups. When each party draws its active members from distinct social groups, members of lower educational and occupational classes have both more opportunity to participate actively and more incentive to do so, since one of the parties is likely to be a vehicle for furthering the special interests of their group. Thus in the United States, where parties are coalitions of diverse groups, party activity does increase with education and occupational status; this is not true in Norway, where a multiparty system allows parties to appeal to more narrow social groups. Furthermore, the more closely a party in either country is connected with lower-class economic organizations, the less important are education and occupation in recruiting party activists. These two factors matter less in the Socialist Party in Norway than in the nonsocialist parties, less in the Democratic Party than in the Republican Party in the United States, and less in the Norwegian Socialist Party than in the American Democratic Party.

Finally, the class nature of a party significantly affects, even in the United States, the extent to which women adherents participate. In parties which appeal more to lower-class groups, a woman's education and occupation have little effect upon whether she is an active member, while in parties oriented more toward the upper classes a woman is quite unlikely to be active unless she is well-educated or has a high status occupation. Thus the generalizations about the type of person who is politically active must be qualified to some extent, at least as far as partisan political participation is concerned.

Social and economic status and level of education not only affect, within the limits just specified, the extent to which a person participates in politics; they also, as is well-known, significantly influence his partisan preferences. Studies of voting in several countries demonstrate what everyone would expect— upper-class voters favor the more conservative parties, which advocate a limited role for the government in managing the economy and providing welfare benefits; and lower-class voters prefer the more liberal or radical parties. But in no country does class correlate perfectly with party; in each case significant numbers of voters cross class lines to vote for a party other than the one which would seem most closely oriented to their class. Are such movements of voters more common in one country than another? Is politics more of a class struggle in some systems than others, and, if so, why?

Comparative research on this subject is extremely limited, chiefly because of a lack of relevant information. Since voting is secret, the extent of class voting can be investigated only if social survey data are available, unless we were to be satisfied with the less reliable technique of ecological correlations.[5] And in few countries have political social surveys been conducted for any length of time. Even in a country as westernized and stable as New Zealand, national opinion polls have been rare.

Thus Alford, in the major study of class voting, was forced to restrict his research to Canada, Australia, Britain, and the United States.[6] One advantage of this limited range was that all the countries included shared a fairly similar political culture and level of economic development. The problem of whether it is valid to compare countries whose political systems are as disparate as those, say, of Denmark and Nigeria, did not arise.

Alford found that class voting was greatest in Britain, somewhat less in Australia, limited in the United States, and lowest in Canada. In Australia religion is a more important factor than class for some Catholics in deciding how they will vote, and thus they do not vote for the Labor Party even though they belong to the lower class. American parties not only draw diverse class support, but in the South their appeal is little related to class. Finally, both religion and region are more significant determinants of the party for which a Canadian votes than is his economic class.

Class voting is related to a sense of national identity. When this is absent, when cultural and economic regionalism is high, and when federalism is not just a constitutional form composed of artificial administrative subunits but is built on a system of distinctive, vigorous states, class voting is low. Economic interests of particular regions as units override the economic interests of particular classes within the regions, so that their interests appear to be the same as those of other classes within the same region and jointly opposed to all classes in other regions. Thus regional voting limits class voting. Religious voting will also reduce class voting unless politics is secularized, unless the sense of national identity is sufficiently strong to make religious belief seem politically irrelevant. If class factors are most important in determining one's vote, then religion and region are relatively unimportant; if support for parties varies little between classes, religion and region are important.

Class voting is also associated with income and availability of education. Per capita income is higher in the United States and Canada, the two countries where class voting is lower, than it is in Australia and Britain. And a greater proportion of the population has had higher education in both Canada and the United States. The point would seem to be that the lower classes have more grievances in Australia and Britain—their income is lower and their opportunity to improve their position through advanced education is more limited. It should not be surprising that politics is fought more along class lines in these two countries.

This conclusion raises the question of whether class voting is declining. The more prosperous a country is the more money it can spend to expand educational opportunity, and the more likely workers are to receive higher wages. All four of these countries are obviously more wealthy than they were twenty years ago. Have improved conditions made the working class less dissatisfied? This question really applies only to Britain and Australia, since class voting is about as low as it can get in Canada and is not marked in the United States. Increased prosperity does not seem to have affected class voting in Britain and Australia significantly. Class voting in Australia has declined—in fact in the 1940s it was greater there than in Britain—but only slightly in the long run. In Britain, on the other hand, it rose until the late 1950s, despite the improvement in economic conditions, and since then has begun to decline.

In Europe greater prosperity and the lessening of class differences has not reduced the electoral support of left or radical parties.[7] These parties have become more moderate—the German Social Democrats have jettisoned their former anticlericalism, their pacifism, and most of their commitment to public ownership of industry; the Nenni Socialists in Italy have moved from being Communist fellow travelers to coalition partners with the Christian Democrats—but they do not seem to be suffering from a massive shift of former supporters toward more conservative parties. If anything, they would appear to have lost supporters to more leftist parties or through abstentions as protests against their moderate policies and relatively ineffective role in coalition governments. The class nature of their support may be shifting, however, even though their total strength has not declined greatly and class voting may be becoming less marked.

One other relevant factor must be noted. The ordering of the four Anglo-American democracies from highest to lowest class voting is the same as their ordering from highest to lowest urbanization. Alford speculates that moving to the city may facilitate class politics by breaking old loyalties. Should this be the case, then the effect of increased incomes and expanded educational opportunities in reducing class voting would be counteracted to some extent. As an economy industrializes and as agriculture mechanizes, people move to the cities. In both the United States and Canada, as well as in most European countries, this shift in population is likely to continue for some time and to support at least some class voting.

The possibility that class voting might increase in the United States will probably disturb many Americans. American political parties have often been praised precisely because they are not class parties but coalitions of diverse groups. Class parties are regarded as being extreme and intransigent in their demands and, therefore, so likely to embitter political conflict that basic consensus can be destroyed. The available evidence little warrants such a belief. Class voting is high in Britain and Australia, but their political systems are as stable and secure as that of the United States. Similarly, the existence of class parties in Scandinavia does not jeopardize the political system. In fact one could as easily argue instead that regional voting threatens political stability at least as much as class voting does. The inability of American political parties to bridge regional differences in the midnineteenth century contributed significantly to the outbreak of the Civil War.[8] And currently, political conflict in the United States certainly would not be less sharp were the Southern Democrats to organize a third party completely separate from the present Democratic Party.

The explosiveness of regional political differences is equally obvious in Canada. French-Canadian resentment of what is felt to be treatment as inferiors by the rest of the country has threatened to erupt, bypassing the constitutional channels for settling political differences, with serious talk that Quebec might secede from Canada and occasional terrorist bombing by French-Canadian extremist groups. As for religious voting, the United States had a glimpse in the 1960 Presidential campaign of how divisive that can be. Thus, if political struggle were fought out in the United States more along class lines, this would not necessarily injure the political process by transforming it into some "foreign" or "un-American" type. Such a development might even make American democracy more vigorous, since, as previously observed, people of lower economic status are more likely to participate actively in politics when parties appeal to more homogeneous social and economic groups.

Parties, the Party System, and the Political System

While personal characteristics are quite important in shaping attitudes toward political activity, they are not the only factors which significantly influence political behavior. Even in a democracy, one disposed to a certain type of political action cannot express his demands on the government through the electoral process entirely without constraint. The party system and the electoral system structure the expression of his demands; they both facilitate and restrict participation in the political process. The voter can choose only among those parties and candidates appearing on the ballot, and he can indicate this choice only in the specified manner—in the United States he votes for only one person for a given office, and the candidate with the greatest number of votes wins.

Some people have questioned whether this single-member, simple-plurality electoral system correctly expresses the electorate's will, since under it a party can easily win a fifth or a quarter of the vote and gain only a handful of seats in the legislature (conceivably a party could win 49 percent of the vote and no seats, but that is extremely unlikely). They feel that public opinion is represented more accurately when the share of seats a party gains in the legislature corresponds closely to the proportion of votes it wins.

Perhaps, however, even this system distorts the voters' desires. If more than two candidates are contesting an election, voters are less constrained if they are permitted to rank the candidates in the order they prefer them rather than being required to select only one. For some time, those interested in constitutional government have debated the merits of various types of electoral systems and have sought to devise more ideal or "just" ways for the electorate to express demands. Their inventiveness has been remarkable—highest remainder proportional representation, highest average proportional representation, alternate vote, cumulative vote, single transferable vote, are only a few examples.[9]

The merit of an electoral system does not rest solely, however, on its ability to accurately reflect popular demands on the government. Equally important is the question of what effect an electoral system has on the party system and the quality of politics generally. Proportional representation has been indicted for so fragmenting the party system that stable, effective government was impossible in Fourth Republic France and Weimar Germany, and for helping the Nazis seize control of the German government. What, then, are the implications of choosing one electoral system or another as a means of enabling the population to express their demands?

The generalization that single-member, simple-plurality electoral systems are conducive to two-party systems, while proportional-representation and double-ballot systems favor multiparty systems is perhaps the most familiar generalization in political science, most recently asserted and extensively defended in Duverger's study of parties and electoral systems. The United States, New Zealand, and Britain all use the first type of system and have two parties; France, Italy, and the Scandinavian countries use the other types and have multiparty systems. The accuracy of this statement obviously depends, however, on how the term *two-party system* is defined.

More than two parties contest elections in Britain; more than two hold seats in the House of Commons. Although the Liberals gain a relatively small share of the vote in Britain, the two major British parties received little more of the popular vote in the 1964 and 1966 elections than did the two main parties in Germany in the 1965 election. Isn't Britain a two-party system? Isn't Germany a multiparty system?

Whatever the answers, reconciling the similarity of major and minor party strengths in the two countries with the fact that one uses proportional representation and the other the single-member, simple-plurality system is difficult, if the latter system is connected with one type of party system and the former with another. Canada provides further conflicting evidence. In recent elections there, the two major parties not only won substantially less of the popular vote than did the two leading German parties, but also less than the two strongest parties in Belgium. Yet Belgium, like Germany, uses proportional representation and Canada the single-member, simple-plurality system.

In view of such evidence you may wonder why anyone ever thought that the single-member, simple-plurality system should produce a two-party system. The argument is that under this system large parties gain a greater share of the seats in the legislature than their proportion of the popular vote warrants, while smaller parties obtain less than their share, since, as previously noted, they may gain a large number of votes in every constituency but seldom outpoll all other parties. Since smaller parties are underrepresented in the legislature, their impact is slight. Their supporters will recognize that continuing to vote for them is futile and will switch to other parties. Thus the small parties will decline still further and eventually only two parties will remain.

Apart from the fact that this argument is not very sound logically, once again the evidence fails to support it.[10] How constituencies are drawn and whether urban areas are underrepresented at the expense of rural areas seems to have a greater impact than does the electoral system on whether a party's share of the seats in the legislature is larger or smaller than its proportion of the vote. Nor is there any systematic evidence that voters desert their preferred party because its reduced legislative strength makes it appear ineffective.

As to why proportional representation should be related to multiparty systems, it is thought to reverse the two effects just discussed. Under such electoral systems, parties receive a share of seats in parliament commensurate with their share of the popular vote and, therefore, their voters will not turn to other parties; every vote helps to win seats and none is wasted, as occurs in a single-member constituency where a small party has no hope of coming first. Proportional representation thus preserves parties which would be eliminated under the single-member, simple-plurality system. Furthermore, it encourages people to form many new parties, since each can expect to win some seats in the legislature even if its share of the total vote nationally is only a few percentage points.

The evidence on this argument is mixed. The number of parties represented in the legislature did increase in the Scandinavian countries, Switzerland, and Belgium after each of these countries adopted proportional representation. None of these countries had had a two-party system prior to that time, however (Denmark even had a four-party system despite using a single-member, simple-plurality electoral system), and the number of parties represented increased by only two or three. In the Netherlands the increase was greater, but has since declined so that now fewer parties hold seats in the legislature than did before the country used proportional representation.

As for Germany, where proportional representation is supposed to have had the most pernicious effect, the number of parties contesting elections did rise substantially when it was adopted, but a smaller percentage of them than under the former electoral system were able to gain seats in parliament. The absolute number of parties represented in the Weimar parliament never exceeded that in the imperial legislature, even allowing for the number of regional parties that were eliminated when Germany's boundaries were altered after World War I. Furthermore, proportional representation appears to save declining parties only temporarily. In the long run, parties whose support is waning continue to lose strength even under this system.

Instead of attempting to argue, as have some political scientists, that single-member, simple-plurality electoral systems cause or "favor" two-party systems, while double-ballot systems and proportional representation encourage multiparty systems, it is more sensible, although rather more obvious and less interesting, to maintain that the party system is causative of the electoral system. When a multiparty system developed despite the absence of proportional representation, the parties found that elections were something of a gamble, since a party's representation in the legislature was only partially related to its ability to win popular support, and a small shift in votes could produce a considerable shift in legislative strength. Thus they changed the electoral system to proportional representation to help reduce the element of risk.

The reverse development seems to be occurring at present in Germany; as the party system moves more toward a two-party type, talk of revising the proportional-representation electoral system to a single-member, simple-plurality type becomes more serious. In either case the parties produce the electoral system, not the electoral system the party system.

To say, however, that proportional representation does not affect the political process is to adopt too extreme a position. It may be one of the factors contributing to the development of an extreme rather than a moderate multiparty system. The latter, which involves a maximum of five parties, operates largely like a two-party system, because where it exists the parties tend to focus on two main points. The extreme system, with its larger number of parties, is fundamentally different, for under it no real alternative government exists. The ruling center coalition may sometimes incline more to the left and other times more to the right, but it always remains in power since the parties congregated around the other two focal points are basically opposed to the governmental system. Politics in such a system is more contentious. Basic consensus among the parties is missing. Party appeals are more likely to be ideological and to be directed to a narrow segment of the population.

The extreme type of multiparty system is likely to occur if proportional representation is introduced before parties are well-organized down to the local level and have become identified with fairly specific policy goals, for then their unity is fragile and they can be fragmented easily. Should universal suffrage be adopted simultaneously with proportional representation, the prospects of developing an extreme, rather than a moderate, multiparty system are even greater. If parties are institutionalized when proportional representation and universal suffrage are introduced, however, they are unlikely to be affected sufficiently to transform a moderate system into an extreme one. Thus in still another context Huntington's point about the need to institutionalize political structures prior to expanding greatly opportunities for political participation is very significant.

Another factor shaping the party system is the level and strength of party identification. As previously noted, considerably fewer people in France than in the United States identify with a political party because fewer fathers discuss politics with or within the hearing of their children. Thus in France a large number of voters are uncommitted to existing parties and are readily available to be mobilized behind a new political group that can momentarily arouse some public interest. In France parties skyrocket out of nowhere, burst into a stunning display of pyrotechnics, and promptly shimmer into oblivion.

Obviously, the kinds of parties functioning in a nation significantly affects the nature of the party system. Large antisystem parties, like the Communists and the Fascists, and church-related parties, unless they are connected so slightly that those of another faith can be party leaders and do not hesitate to vote for the party, are very likely to make a multiparty system extreme rather than moderate.

Thus far this discussion of the factors related to various types of party systems has dealt almost exclusively with competitive party systems in developed democracies. Noncompetitive party systems also need to be examined as well to discover what factors are associated with these systems. The attempt to do so oversimplifies to some extent, even if limited to African nations, since it lumps into a single category—noncompetitive system—political systems as diverse from each other as they are from competitive, Western systems.[11] Nonetheless, whether all parties but one are outlawed, or whether all parties but one, despite freedom from legal constraints on their activities, have virtually no share in political power and governmental positions, party systems in most African countries are not as competitive as in the more developed democracies. Furthermore, these countries share some basic similarities of political development; thus, they may be grouped together for the purpose of seeking factors related to less competitive party systems.

The type of traditional authority structure which existed in each of these countries has shaped its type of party system. Where this structure was stronger and more adaptable, centralizing power into a single hierarchical party was more difficult. The vitality of the traditional authority structures obviously depends in part on the way they were treated by colonial rulers. Coleman and Rosberg have argued that in general the British tended to protect traditional authorities and to use them as units of local government, while the French sought to destroy the traditional order. From this they conclude that establishing one-party systems was easier in former French colonies than in former British colonies and that the former countries could be more readily unified into a self-conscious national entity.

The data from A *Cross-Polity Survey*, however, only partially confirms this argument. The majority of former French colonies which became independent after 1914 are one-party systems (68 percent), while the great majority of former British colonies independent since then are not (17 percent).[12] This is true also of only African former colonies—76 per cent of the French are one-party systems and only 33 percent of the British are. Sectionalism is moderate or negligible much more frequently in former French than in former British colonies (86 to 58 percent), although it is one or the other in more than half of the former British colonies. But the *Cross-Polity* data show no strong relation between former colonial ruler and the extent of political integration in a country. Clearly the policy of the former colonial ruler toward traditional authority structures is only one factor affecting national unity, and its effect may be offset by other influences.

A second factor influencing the type of party system in African nations is their experience with colonial government. The relation between the indigenous people and the colonial rulers was rather authoritarian and bureaucratic, a relation of command and obedience rather than of participation. The proper political structure thus appeared to be a single, hierarchical system.

The fragile unity of the African nations has also helped to encourage a preference for the one-party system. Political leaders concerned to enhance the international status and importance of their countries have been willing to tolerate little diversity, since any dissent seems to threaten to fragment the nation. Thus competitive party systems have been shunned as jeopardizing national unity. Furthermore, a single-party system has appeared to be more conducive to developing the economy rapidly. Partisan debate about the government's plans for economic development is seen as retarding growth.

The desire for rapid economic growth is related to another factor favoring a one-party system—communist doctrine. Although few African political leaders are communists, the Soviet Union's rapid economic growth has convinced many of them that it offers a model for economic development which is more relevant to their circumstances than is capitalism, even of the contemporary welfare variety. Then too, they are attracted by communist ideology's denunciation of imperialism. Thus although they may not go so far as to create a totalitarian political system, they may imitate the Soviet Union to the extent of establishing a one-party system.

Finally, in many cases a one-party system exists not because a deliberate effort was made to establish it, but because it had already developed by the time of independence. To be effective, independence movements had to mobilize widespread popular support; fragmented efforts allowed colonial powers to apply the tactic of divide and rule. Most of the credit for obtaining independence went to the independence movement in each country. As a result, their prestige often was so great that they overshadowed all other political groups. Therefore, in most African countries the one-party system undoubtedly appears as "natural" as the two-party system does in the United States.

As these comments indicate, the role parties play in a nation's political process varies from one type of political system to another. Among the significant functions performed by political parties in democratic systems are offering candidates for election, debating public policy, coordinating the activity of governmental organs, and stimulating political participation. Wide as the scope of party activity is, parties do not monopolize political behavior— they are not the only channels through which one can participate in politics—nor do they actually rule a country, however much they may influence political leaders. Therefore, some people have thought that parties are most important, reach the peak of their power, in totalitarian systems. The Communist Party is frequently said, for example, to rule the Soviet Union. Totalitarian regimes do emphasize parties and movements more than democratic systems do, but even in countries of the former type, parties are not the sole governing structure.[13]

The extent of direct party control depends in part, of course, on the specific circumstances in a country. The Nazis, being an economically conservative and nationalistic movement, did not seek to transform Germany as completely as did the Communists in the Soviet Union. Thus in Germany the bureaucrats, the military elite, and the economic leaders were willing to cooperate with the Nazis, enabling the party to attain its goals without direct control of all elements of society.

In the Soviet Union, on the other hand, cooperation between elements of the old order and the Communist Party was out of the question, except in cases when the Communists, for lack of essential technical skills, had to coerce assistance. To illustrate, in the civil war against the counterrevolutionaries, Communist armies were led by Czarist officers whose families were held hostage to insure that their military abilities were applied as skillfully as possible to defeat the enemies of the new regime. The Communists could expect little voluntary assistance from the old elite. Despite these different conditions, however, the Communist Party has not been the only power center in the Soviet Union, has not been *the* ruling group any more than the Nazi party was in Germany. The same has been true in China.

Regardless of the circumstances prevailing in these totalitarian countries, the nature of their parties has been such as to make them unfit to function as a ruling group. In all three countries the party has been too large to govern efficiently, too arbitrary and nonselective in recruiting and promoting to insure a supply of capable people, too frequently purged to maintain morale at a sufficiently high level, and too poorly organized and frequently reorganized to be effective as a governing organ. The party does indoctrinate the population and prevents potential opponents from forming opposition organs. And it does help to control the military and economic structures. But the police also perform this function. Furthermore, all three of these elements have independent power of their own which can influence government policy.

The totalitarian system, then, is not a monolith. Rather, it is composed of a number of competing, overlapping hierarchies each of which serves to some extent as a control group over the others. The totalitarian leader maximizes his power not by heading a single structure, but by being independent of any organization and being able to dominate all power centers. If a single structure were the key power center, the dictator's control over the system would be tenuous, since his opponents could overthrow him by winning in only one arena. When his power is based on several centers, however, he is more secure, because his opponents cannot concentrate their efforts on only one point. The totalitarian party is more likely to compete with, obstruct, or, for mutual defense, cooperate with the governmental bureaucracy than it is to control it as a ruling group.

The role of a party in a totalitarian system contrasts sharply with that of parties in democratic systems. In a democracy, although interest groups do contact governmental organs frequently, their policy goals are relatively limited and they do not seek to control and direct the government in all its operations. Thus a great deal of interest-group activity is channeled through the party system as groups attempt to get parties to adopt candidates and policies favorable to their views. The parties to a varying extent—depending upon their number and type—help to focus the demands expressed by other groups and furnish the personnel to operate the government.

By contrast, in the totalitarian system the party virtually becomes one of a number of interest groups, each of which seeks to decide and direct public policy not only to further what would seem to be its immediate areas of interest but to control all matters. Each group has its own procedures for recruiting and training personnel and each provides some of the political system's decision-making elite.

Parties also function as simply one of a number of competing groups in systems which are not totalitarian. In Central America, for example, the struggle for political power among groups with power potential takes place largely outside of the party system.[14] Parties are the instrument which the rising middle class in these countries is attempting to use to enter the process of authoritative decision making. Although these parties in their goals and values are middle class, their power capability, which keeps them from being ignored entirely, is their potential for mobilizing mass support. They have not yet sufficiently realized this potential, however, to be unconstrained. The established power groups will permit the parties to operate only so long as they do not jeopardize the traditional elite by seeking basic reforms. Thus although parties in these countries help to democratize the political system by bringing new groups into the political process, they can do little to improve significantly the living conditions of most people.

While political parties in any political system can help to legitimate the system, this function is especially important in relatively new nations, where the government's authority may not be widely accepted.[15] In many of these countries, past experience with colonial government has led the people to regard government as an oppressor. When parties put the prestige which they won in the fight for independence behind the government, they help to make it respectable. Also, since many of these parties are better organized at the grass-roots level than is the government, their contact with the people is more direct. They can help to integrate the population into the political process.

Contrary to what political leaders in most new nations believe, however, a one-party system is not necessarily the most effective instrument for this purpose. Competitive parties may be able to involve a diverse number of groups in the political process more readily than can a single party, and make them feel a greater stake in continuing the existing system because they more truly have a voice in it. Furthermore, attempting to integrate a nation through a single-party system has at least one major drawback—the party becomes excessively identified with the government. It tends, as a result, to lose its independent vitality and people are less willing than formerly to participate in its activities. This development precludes it from performing effectively the significant task of recruiting new, skillful personnel for political positions.

Political Participation through Interest Groups

Another major channel through which demands for authoritative decisions are expressed and structured or focused are interest groups. Although the type of group most active in politics and the methods they employ vary from one political system to another, groups are involved significantly in the decision-making process in all countries. Groups play an important role even in dictatorial systems, for, as I pointed out in discussing parties, these systems are not monoliths. Different factions and groups oppose each other in a struggle to have the conflicting policies which each prefers made binding officially.

The activities of interest groups in the United States have been studied for some time, at first as political maladies and subsequently as legitimate, even desirable, behavior in a democratic system. Research on interest groups in other countries lagged behind, however, until well after World War II. Only in recent years have political scientists studied particular interests in other countries, such as the British Medical Association and business groups in France, or the activities of interest groups generally in a country other than the United States.[16] Furthermore, they have seldom gone beyond this to study interest groups comparatively. Even books dealing with groups in several countries tend to proceed country by country with little effort to apply an integrated conceptual framework rigorously.[17]

The studies of particular interests and individual countries demonstrate that the methods interest groups use differ considerably from one country to another. In Great Britain, members of the House of Commons may be interest-group officers and accept campaign contributions from trade unions, corporations, or any group; furthermore, they are permitted to receive periodic payments from interest groups to supplement their legislative salaries—a virtual retainer for their influence since they may voice their groups' views during Parliamentary debate and seek to obtain legislation which the groups desire. Such a close relation between a legislator and an interest group would not be allowed in the United States. Yet most British interest groups devote more time to lobbying bureaucrats and less to attempting to influence legislators than do American interest groups. Campaigns to write your legislator are not a popular tactic with British interest groups. Because until recently the House of Commons had no specialist legislative committees, there have been no committee hearings at which representatives of interest groups could testify, as they do in the United States, in an effort to demonstrate the need for legislation they desired. Tight party discipline in Britain greatly restricts the power of the individual legislator; therefore, interest groups are more concerned to win the support of bureaucrats and Cabinet ministers. In a sense interest groups behave no differently in Britain from the way they do in the United States; in each country they focus their efforts on those structures and people holding the greatest power. Since the locus of power in Britain differs from that in the United States, groups in the two countries employ different tactics. Their goals, however, and thus the function they perform in the political process, are the same.

Clearly, then, continuing to detail the variety of techniques employed by pressure groups in a string of countries would be unlikely to enhance your understanding of groups. In the absence of a conceptual framework to give meaning to such information, I merely would be offering a series of unrelated facts rather than fertile hypotheses. The preferable course is to distinguish generally among various types of interest groups and indicate in which political systems these types are most prominent.

The informal interest group is usually the most inchoate and ephemeral. The appearance of an issue on the government's agenda stimulates some people's interest and they seek the help of others to oppose or support it. They may try to persuade others to visit or write to a governmental official, or to sign a petition, or to help arrange or at least attend a public meeting to discuss the issue. In some ways the channel through which they direct their efforts can hardly be termed a group at all; they have not created an elaborately or permanently organized structure. Yet they are not acting individually; they have chosen a group strategy.

This type of group activity seems to be especially American, in particular at the local level.[18] More than half the Americans interviewed for *The Civic Culture* indicated that they would form an informal group in trying to influence their local governments, while only a third of the British and a quarter of the Mexican respondents favored this strategy, which won still smaller acceptance in Germany and Italy. As for attempting to influence the national goverment, the proportion of respondents who would organize an informal group remained greatest in the United States, although it dropped to 29 percent. Only 18 percent in Britain and Mexico preferred this method, with the proportion in Germany and Italy again lower still. Almond and

Verba believe that this preference in the United States for the informal group strategy is related to a relatively high level of trust in others and a low intensity of partisan conflict, which dispose Americans to feel that they can cooperate with others.

The appearance of an issue on the government's agenda may evoke formal as well as informal interest groups. Formal groups are less casual; their structure is more explicit and their procedures more regular. In some instances, of course, the formal groups interested in a particular issue were organized before the issue became prominent. Formal groups active in politics may have been created primarily for that purpose, such as a group favoring the abolition of capital punishment, or to achieve other aims, such as the American Medical Association. They may be concerned with a single issue or a broad range of policy.

Since almost invariably formal groups are better organized, financially and numerically stronger, and more likely to have developed contacts with public officials than informal groups are, they would seem to provide the potentially most effective channel for influencing the government. Yet few people in the five *Civic Culture* nations conceived of the groups to which they belonged this way. Interestingly, in contrast with the findings about attitudes toward informal group strategy, national differences were very slight. The proportion of respondents saying they would work through a formal group to influence local government ranged only from 1 percent in Italy to 5 percent in Germany with the other three nations coming in between, and from 2 percent in Italy to 7 percent in Germany for efforts to influence the national government. This is not to say that interest groups are unimportant in these countries—since they have the assets noted, they are considerably more influential than informal groups— but to note that despite the significant role which formal interest groups play in the political process, most people do not see the groups to which they belong as channels through which they can express effectively their demands on the government. They think much more in terms of contacting a politician themselves.

The type of interest group I have been discussing can be

labeled associational to distinguish it from two other types—nonassociational and institutional. Groups of the former type, although they may be active in politics, exist totally apart from any desire to exert political influence. One belongs to them not because he chooses to but by virtue of what he is. I refer not to trade unions in factories having a union shop nor to organizations like the NAACP, for both of these are associational groups. An example of a nonassociational group would be one based on ethnic or racial distinctions where membership in the group is so automatic as to be unquestioned, as in a tribe. Institutional interest groups, like nonassociational groups and some associational groups, do not have as their primary purpose the function of expressing demands upon the government. Unlike these groups, however, institutional interest groups are organizations formally established as part of the political system. When the Pentagon sends Air Force officers to convince Congress that more money needs to be appropriated to build a superbomber, the Pentagon is behaving as an interest group. Yet the type of group involved in this activity obviously cannot be equated with a group of people who decide to write their Congressman or with the National Association of Manufacturers. The Pentagon has a status different from such groups; it is part of the institutional structure of the American political system. Therefore, groups of this nature need to be distinguished as institutional interest groups.

The prominence of associational interest groups in the political process is related to a country's level of economic development, provided that such groups are free to organize.[19] When they are not, as in the Soviet Union, they have little political impact, of course, even though the country is relatively developed. Major political forces in developed democracies, associational interest groups are only moderately significant in Latin America and are unimportant in the Near East, Asia, and Africa. Trade unions, for example, are poorly organized, badly financed, and lack capable leaders, in Asia and Africa.[20] Although they are more active in politics than in economics—they are little concerned with such functions as bargaining with employers over wages and working conditions—they do not provide a channel through which workers can communicate demands to the government. Instead they function as instruments of the government to control the people by propagandizing them.

When, therefore, a society has not modernized sufficiently far to enervate traditional ties, nonassociational groups are more significant. Relatively unimportant in developed democracies, groups of this type are the dominant interests in African politics. They play a major role also in Asia, while in the Near East, although important in the past, their impact has declined as nations in this area urbanize and industrialize. In Latin America they remain significant primarily only for Indians.

The type of interest groups most common in a country greatly affects its political process. Where associational groups are weak or nonexistent, people may be forced to resort to riots or other mob action as the only means of expressing their demands, especially if political parties also are little developed. National leaders cannot gauge accurately from such violent outbursts how much support various demands have. Thus it is difficult for them to reconcile conflicting demands in such a way as to satisfy most people. This difficulty remains when interests are expressed through nonassociational groups, not because of the problem of measuring support, but because compromise is hard to obtain. The interests of a nonassociational group are tied up with its very existence as a structure playing an integral role in its members' lives; thus it is unlikely to be satisfied with a partial granting of its demands. In an effort to cope with these problems, political leaders appeal for support on the basis of a nondivisive policy like nationalism, although in some countries even this strategy does not succeed in uniting the people.

Whether institutional interest groups are important politically does not seem to depend on the level of economic development. The bureaucracy is an influential group in France as well as in Thailand. Although the bureaucracy is a significant political force in most developing countries, in Latin America (except for Brazil) administrative structure usually is weak and, therefore, the bureaucracy has little political importance. The Catholic Church, however, plays a major political role in many Latin American countries as well as in Italy. As for a third subtype of institutional interest group, the military, while the extent of its intervention into politics and the methods it employs differ considerably from one system to another, is a prominent interest group in the United States as well as in the Soviet Union and Turkey. The political influence of the military is least significant in Africa, although the bureaucracy, another subtype of institutional interest group, is an influential force. Thus no pattern of prominence for institutional groups as a general type emerges.

Solely in terms of physical strength, the military is the most powerful organization in most countries. This fact warrants more detailed consideration of this subtype of institutional interest group, especially in nations in which other political structures—parliaments, parties, and associational interest groups—are not firmly established.[21]

The reasons for military participation in politics vary, of course. Although in some instances the motive is little more than personal ambition, other factors are usually involved. The military is naturally concerned to maintain its morale; to do this requires the respect of its countrymen. It is hardly likely to win respect if it is poorly equipped and appears impotent, so it may intervene in politics to enhance its status. The Latin American military has had few wars in which to demonstrate its abilities; it lacks a glorious military tradition; and it has gained little popular support because it has been used to suppress the population. The only way for military officers to gain prestige was through involvement in politics so that rank would become a symbol of political power. In some countries the military has been recruited primarily from a particular class or region and intervenes in politics to protect the interests of those sectors. Or the military may act to defend the interests of the entire country. It is one of the chief symbols of national sovereignty; its function is to defend the state from attack; it is above partisan politics. Such thoughts encourage the military to conceive of itself as having a unique duty of caring for the national interest; thus, it may feel impelled to clean up corrupt politics, break political deadlock, or prevent the disintegration of the political system. Only through its action will the political and economic systems be ordered, efficient, and disciplined, like the military itself.

The military's opportunity to be politically influential is greatest when the government is most dependent on it. This may be because the government has little legitimacy and must rely upon the military in order to maintain power, or because the country is involved in a war. Often a military takeover occurs when a country is so sharply divided that it appears to be on the verge of civil war. This development is a serious possibility not only in developing countries; France only narrowly avoided a military coup in 1958 when it was so divided over the war against the Algerian rebels that it seemed to face civil war.

The extent to which the military participates in politics is restricted significantly by the public attitude toward the military and the political system. In some countries the population is committed strongly to the existing political structures and favors a limited role in politics for the military. In such cases the military can do little more than function as one of a number of interest groups. When the population disagrees about the procedures for transferring power or about who should wield authoritative power, or when it is so weak that its opinions can be disregarded, the military can govern indirectly, allowing civilians to retain political offices and some power but setting the conditions within which the government will be allowed to operate, or it can become the actual ruling group.

The military is especially likely to play one or the other of these two roles when no tradition exists of separating the military from civilian government. The influence of Turkey on the Near East and North Africa established the contrary tradition of rule by military officers. Not surprisingly, direct or indirect military rule is more common in this area than in Asia or Sub-Sahara Africa. Almost all the countries in the latter two areas were at one time ruled by foreign powers, but, unlike the countries in the

Near East and North Africa, they usually did not live under military government. Also, except for Sudan and Senegal, the colonial rulers of Sub-Sahara Africa did not create indigenous armies within the boundaries of single colonies. Those forces which did exist, therefore, could not provide an established post-independence military for countries in this area. Thus the military, young and weak, has had little political influence so far. The experience of countries in Asia, the Near East, and North Africa indicates, however, that the longer a developing country is independent, the more likely the military is to be involved in politics. The recent intervention of the military into Nigerian politics may simply be a preview of the developments to be expected in Sub-Sahara Africa.

In Latin America, on the other hand, the military is increasingly inclined to rule indirectly rather than through an overt take-over. As the economy develops in this area, as the people become more politically aware, and as associational groups become more prevalent and firmly established, suppressing or disregarding the people becomes much more difficult.

Also, as the military becomes more professional, being an officer becomes a full-time career, unlike the situation in the past when military leaders were daring and gifted amateurs whose main occupation and means of support were in the civilian sector. Professional military men are less suited for governing directly because they lack the skills of negotiating and compromising among conflicting groups and the knowledge of public interests and needs which are essential for successfully performing the political role. Eschewing the coup for indirect rule or even the role of one of a number of interest groups need not mean a decline in the military's power. The government's expanded role in managing the economy and supplying welfare services has increased greatly the number of government posts. In Latin America military men fill many of these newly created positions; thus they continue to exercise considerable power.

The military in most developing countries is a channel for middle- and lower-middle-class participation in politics. It is fairly common for the fathers of officers to have been minor government employees or school teachers. Since the key positions in these countries' economies are frequently held by foreigners, a military career provides one of the few alternatives to politics as a means of social mobility and a route to power. Where entry into politics is restricted, the middle class may be forced to participate through the military.

Military leaders are more nearly a representative cross-section of the population in Sub-Sahara Africa, for the missionary schools which provided most primary and secondary education there were not limited to particular classes. Nonetheless, groups employed in the more modern sectors of the economy were more likely to be near a school and thus even there the middle class is somewhat overrepresented among military leaders.

Therefore, in most developing countries the military is not concerned to maintain the power of the conservative, landed upper class. Although officers are recruited disproportionately from rural areas—the areas which would be expected to be most traditional—the military frequently favors social and economic reform. In many cases the military is the most modern institution in a developing country. Its leaders recognize that its strength is likely to be jeopardized by traditional beliefs and behaviors in the nonmilitary parts of society.

The Latin American military traditionally was identified with the landed upper class. However, as the military became more professional and bureaucratized, and as its need for managerial and scientific skills grew, a different type of person began to be recruited into military careers. Thus, although many of the top officers are still connected with the old order, the young officers, especially since the end of World War II, come from the middle class, drawn initially from the rural or small-town upper middle class and subsequently from the urban middle class. In fact, as the development of the economy encourages the well-educated to seek profitable and prestigious careers in other fields, expanded educational opportunity permits the lower classes to qualify for military schools so that even they are supplying an increasing number of officers. Since the more recently recruited officers are better educated than their predecessors, they are less oriented toward perpetuating traditional society and more receptive to modernization.

Regardless of the military's class composition, when it is most professional and when the country is most developed, its interest in industralization is greatest. The officers' interest in technological progress disposes them to accept a shift in political power away from the landed interest. This does not mean that they have become instead the protectors of the industrialists. The more professional officers have not been recruited from industrial families and, having received a managerial or bureaucratic outlook from their training, they are not opposed to the government's playing a major role in the economy.

These differences in class and training have created tensions within the military and help to explain why at times in Latin America reformist military regimes have been succeeded by conservative military rule as first one faction of the armed forces and then another is dominant. The crucial point is that the Latin American military can no longer be regarded as an instrument of the landed class; it is more nearly aligned with the urban middle classes than with any other sector of the population, and in this regard has come to resemble the military in most other developing areas.

Any system's political process is significantly affected by the way in which structures channeling demands to authoritative decision makers function. In many Western democracies, parties help to keep political struggle within peaceful limits by reconciling the diverse interests expressed on key political issues through a wide variety of associational groups into a limited number of policy alternatives, none of which greatly alienates any sizable segment of the population. By devising generally acceptable compromises, the groups serve to provide the consensus essential for political stability. Their function is coalition building. Although British interest groups tend more than do American to deal directly with bureaucrats rather than to channel their demands through parties as such, the British party system does serve to structure political debate by aggregating opinion around a few main alternatives. British parties, like American, help to focus the interests expressed in their political system.

As their number increases, parties are less able to perform this essential focusing function successfully. Coalition building especially is difficult in the extreme, rather than the moderate, multiparty system. Appealing ideologically to narrow segments of the population, parties in this type of system do little to build up consensus. Introducing proportional representation before parties have been institutionalized, or implementing it at the same time as greatly expanding the franchise through granting universal suffrage, is likely to fragment parties so greatly as to produce an extreme multiparty system. Thus in some cases measures that would seem to enhance popular participation in politics may have a negative impact upon the political system.

The poor development of associational interest groups also hinders coalition building. In transitional systems such groups are usually so weak that they tend to serve more as a means for the political leaders to make demands upon and control the people rather than the reverse, which is their function in Western democracies. Since these groups do not function to express popular demands, political leaders encounter greater difficulty in attempting to assess the level of support for various policy alternatives. And gaining the assent of a sizable coalition of interests is more difficult when nonassociational, rather than associational, groups dominate the political process.

Obtaining voluntary consent for authoritative decisions in transitional systems and totalitarian regimes is a problem also because the role of parties contrasts with that in Western two-party and moderate multiparty systems. Demands are not processed typically through party structures. Parties tend to be only one of a number of structures competing for control of political power. When not ignored, interests are likely to be aggregated coercively by a small group of politically irresponsible rulers.

The poor development of association groups and parties in

transitional systems makes institutional interest groups especially significant channels for expressing demands, although institutional groups are by no means confined to such systems. With entry into politics restricted, as is often the case in these systems, institutional groups can help to broaden the base of participation in politics by bringing other segments of the population, especially the middle class, into the political process. Thus, for example, a politically active military cannot be condemned automatically as an antidemocratic characteristic in transitional systems, since it frequently brings into politics an otherwise excluded middle class.

While the opportunities for political participation vary from one type of system to another, in any system the politically active are those who are better off, those who have a higher income and a more prestigious occupation and who are better educated than most people in their country. One of the principal exceptions to this occurs when parties are class-based and socio-economic status is not as great a determinant of whether one is active in a political party. Whether parties are based on relatively narrow social groups or are able to draw support across class lines depends on the balance between feelings of national identity and regionalism, the degree of urbanization, the secularization of politics, the level of wealth, and the breadth of educational opportunity. Although class politics would appear to be a means for broadening political participation by reducing the barrier of low socio-economic status to party activity, some fear that politics of this type would be so divisive that it would impair the coalition-building function. Yet class-based politics has no greater potential for destroying consensus than does regionally or religiously based politics. The extreme multiparty system which does hamper coalition building derives not from class politics but from a mistiming of proportional representation and universal suffrage.

Clearly, then, the nature of the structures available for channeling demands are a major factor in shaping the quality and style of politics in any political system. They, as well as personal characteristics, determine who participates in politics.

Chapter 5

Policy-making
and Implementing Structures

The Contrast between Institutions and Structures

In older, more traditional texts this chapter would have been called "The Machinery of Government" or something similar; it would have been divided into several sections; and it would have taken up the bulk of the book. For the focal point is those bodies, agencies, organizations which make laws, issue regulations, command people to behave in certain ways, see that these orders are obeyed, and try those who do not comply.

My main concern, however, is not to describe, as would have been done in the past, the legal institutions most commonly found in a number of nations. Instead, having discussed in the last chapter those political structures whose primary function analytically is to express and focus demands, I will now examine not the narrow topic of "The Machinery of Government," but rather those structures which prescribe to what extent through what means these demands are to be granted, and which implement these prescriptions.

To state this chapter's concern in these terms is not to indulge in semantic games. The institutional emphasis is at once both concrete and abstract. It is concrete in the sense of being concerned with the legal or constitutional properties of a particular organ or agency; it is abstract in thinking of this organ almost as a Platonic form divorced from the context, the environment, in which it operates. To focus on structures is not to study machines, not even machines in operation. Rather it is to analyze how those who are part of a structure relate both to each other and to those who are outside the structure. It is not that the one approach is concerned with rules and procedures, while the other ignores these. The difference instead is that the one approach is satisfied largely with examining explicit rules and procedures, while the other also includes, and particularly emphasizes, implicit behavioral modes.

A structure, then, is not a concrete organ; it is a system of interactions, a system of roles, which are the values people associate with particular positions or statuses and the behavior they expect from those occupying positions. A political structure not only is a system—that is, its elements are interdependent—but it also is itself a subsystem of the broader political system which encompasses all of a society's political structures. To focus on structures, therefore, is to recognize that the phenomena one is studying affect and are affected by other systems of behavior; it is to study the phenomena as part of an interrelated whole.

Deciding to use different terms, then, is not just a matter of taste. Rather it is evidence of, and is necessitated by, conceiving of the political process in a new way, of adopting a new perspective. Just as some cubist paintings by reversing the traditional perspective of visual art require us to think of them differently from the way we would other types of paintings, evaluate them by different standards, and use different terms in attempting verbally to express their impact on us, so also a new approach to communicating about government and politics requires to some extent a new vocabulary. Furthermore, the cubist would argue that this approach allows him to express something—a message, a feeling, or an esthetic vision—which he otherwise could not express and which probably is unexpressible through any other approach. So also in political science one adopts a new approach not for the sake of doing something new, but because he has come to feel the existing approaches do not permit him to investigate adequately the significant aspects of the political process. Perhaps they focus attention on the wrong problems—problems which, even if solved, would do little to further understanding. Or perhaps they encourage only superficial, largely descriptive study rather than more penetrating analytical research. These are some of the failings of "The Machinery of Government" approach. One purpose of this chapter is to demonstrate why concentrating narrowly on legal institutions is an inadequate approach to the study of comparative politics.

By no means every political scientist who stresses the importance of institutions is content to describe simple-mindedly a given constitution's provisions. Some may even grant that role expectations and interactions are significant variables, but will argue that these are the product of institutional arrangements. To some extent this certainly is true. What must be emphasized, however, is that role expectations and behavior do not derive solely, or even primarily, from legal institutions. Furthermore, the effect of institutions is not automatic. The same type of legal institutions exist in political systems which function very differently. Institutions may be the rock upon which the barnacles of role expectations and behavior incrust themselves, and institutional reform may lead to changes in role expectations and behavior, yet necessary relations between particular types of institutions and role expectations and behavior have not been established. This is why constitutional tinkering is likely to be a futile endeavor, a point I will discuss further in the following section.

Before turning to this matter, however, I must emphasize that to say that this chapter discusses those structures upon which demands are focused is not to suggest that they should be conceived of as passive, capable only of reacting to external stimuli, like a movie projector which must wait for someone to feed a reel of film into it and turn on its motor before it is able to produce a show. Not uncommonly, demands for authoritative decisions originate within governmental bodies; this is why institutional interest groups had to be among the structures included in the preceding chapter.

Nor am I suggesting that the political process actually progresses through a series of sharply distinct phases each characterized by only one type of activity present in that phase alone. Demands continue to be expressed and focused while prescriptions are being made and implemented. Nonetheless, structures which can act authoritatively for an entire society are distinguishable from those which can only importune. While many of the former qualify as part of the traditional "Machinery of Government," others do not. In some systems the effective power to make authoritative decisions is exercised by a political party, and the governmental institutions can do little more than perform a ritual. This is still another reason why it is preferable to focus on structures rather than legal institutions.

The Chimera of Constitutional Tinkering

While emphasis upon legal institutions is no longer the mechanistic approach it once was, the belief that legal institutions are the primary causal variable in politics remains strong. Faith in the utility of constitutional tinkering seems to have abated little.[1] Those who persist in following the gleam of the more perfect constitution include not only university professors, who are frequently dismissed as "ivory-tower intellectuals" whose work is seldom relevant to the real world. The supposedly more realistic and practical politicians have been even less willing to relinquish their belief in the supreme importance of institutional arrangements and tend to be even more suspicious of noninstitutional political research than are most political scientists. A number of political organizations have commissioned opinion surveys; nonetheless, most politicians remain convinced that they can gain a more accurate knowledge of public opinion simply by reading their mail and talking with a few of their constituents.

The drafting of the Basic Law, or constitution, of West Germany after World War II illustrates well the unquenchable faith in constitutional engineering. During the 1930s and 1940s scholarly writings averred that Article 48 of the Weimar constitution, which allowed the German President to suspend basic political rights in an emergency, was one of the principal factors in the fall of the Republic to Nazism. Hitler could not have gone as far as he did, ran the argument, had these basic rights not been suspended. That Hitler, who regarded international agreements as mere scraps of paper to be torn up whenever convenient, would have deferred to a constitution and allowed it to thwart his political plans is an utterly implausible idea. Yet the drafters of the Basic Law were so convinced that Article 48 was a dangerous constitutional defect that they refused to grant the present German federal government any emergency powers, despite the obvious evidence that the governments of even established democracies like Britain and the United States have required special powers to cope with international and domestic crises and at times have been forced to acquire these by procedures of rather dubious legality.

Rather than being solved, the problem really had only been sidestepped; it appeared again on the German political agenda of the late 1960s as a matter of considerable controversy. The need for widespread consensus on the proposals to eliminate this gap in the government's powers helped impel Germany's two major parties, the Christian Democrats and the Socialists, to join in a Grand Coalition. The entry of the main opposition party into the Government meant that only one-tenth of the members of parliament were not supporters of the Government. Whether this situation will so restrict and enfeeble the channels through which legitimate dissent can be expressed that many Germans will turn to extremist, neo-Nazi parties in an effort to call the Government to account is uncertain, but not inconceivable. Were this to occur, the belief that institutional arrangements are of paramount importance would have helped to produce precisely the result the constitutional engineers were seeking to avoid.

The faith that proper institutional arrangements can forestall dictatorship also led the drafters of the Basic Law to devise some procedures which had not been included in the Weimar constitution; the most innovative of these is the constructive vote of no confidence found in Article 81. Reacting to both French and German experience with indecisive government, the product of short-lived cabinets due to shifting coalitions in multiparty parliaments, the drafters provided that a cabinet could be removed from office only if the parliament was simultaneously able to agree upon a successor to the incumbent Chancellor. This requirement, it was thought, would prevent negative coalitions of, say, the extreme right and left—allies able to agree only upon their desire to oust the existing cabinet and who lacked sufficient common ground to remain united in support of a new cabinet to fill the void left by the defeated one. Two decades of stable and democratic government in West Germany have convinced some political scientists that this is a very sound modification of the classical parliamentary system.

Yet for all its effect, the constructive vote of no confidence might just as well have been omitted from the Basic Law. It never has been used: the German parliament never has gone so far as to defeat the Government on a vote of confidence. Some may argue that this provision has helped to prevent such defeats because the Government's potential opponents, speculating that they will not be able to remain united sufficiently to choose a new Chancellor, abandon any effort to defeat the Government. To be valid, this argument requires specific evidence from the writings or speeches of, or interviews with, a considerable number of German legislators that they have in fact weighed this requirement's possible effects in deciding to what extent they will oppose the Government; until this exists, the argument can be only conjecture. Unless time travel becomes science fact instead of fiction, refuting one who asserts that failure to have done something which actually has been done would have altered circumstances significantly is impossible, for the original situation cannot be restored to allow the choice of this different alternative.

I am not denying that German government has been stable and effective, but rather am suggesting that this accomplishment can be explained better by factors other than institutional reform. More interesting than Article 81 itself is the striking fact that it has been unnecessary. To a considerable extent the sharp decrease in the number of parties electing members to parliament and the concomitant growth of the Christian Democrats so that they either have held or have been close to holding a majority of seats have enabled the German Government to avoid defeat on votes of confidence. And this, rather than Article 81, is what has produced stable and effective government in Germany.

Why the party system has so evolved must itself be explained, however. Although an institutional reform—an electoral law designed to weaken minor parties' parliamentary representation —probably has had some effect, the more fundamental change is the German voters' new willingness to coalesce primarily behind two parties. The voters apparently conceive of the role of parties in a parliamentary democracy quite differently from the way they did during the Weimar Republic. In other words, a major structural change has occurred in the German party system. But this change in role expectation has little to do with legal reforms. This altered voting behavior is related, in turn, to these two parties' tendency to become more pragmatic and policy-oriented in their electoral appeals and less concerned with ideology. Discovering why the parties have modified their styles would require a study of German political culture, especially the impact of the Nazi experience upon the political values of the present political elite. Clearly, factors other than institutional reform have been most significant in producing political stability in postwar Germany.

Regardless of how nations arrange their political institutions, the growth of executive power is virtually universal in the twentieth century. In a parliamentary system the executive supposedly is restrained by its dependence on the legislature. Being fused with the legislature, rather than being autonomous, the executive can be voted out of office at any time; therefore, it must constantly curry favor with the legislature and do nothing to which the legislature objects. Instances of parliamentary systems in which the executive generally was at the legislature's mercy, thus seeming to confirm this argument, are not difficult to find—Germany under the Weimar Republic and Third and Fourth Republic France, for example. In the great majority of contemporary parliamentary systems, however, the situation differs. Although the executive is not unchecked, its power has so expanded in the twentieth century that it controls the legislature, rather than the reverse.

While eschewing a parliamentary system and creating instead a separation-of-powers system, the American founding fathers also were seeking to avoid the danger of executive dominance. They believed that this goal could best be secured by dividing powers among several largely independent governmental institutions, thereby preventing any institution from accumulating sufficient strength to threaten liberty and enabling each organ to limit the actions of the others. The fact that the American Congress is recognized widely as the world's most powerful legislature—the one whose influence in making authoritative policy decisions has given least ground to executive advances—might seem to suggest that the founding fathers were able to devise institutions better suited than parliamentary ones to the achievement of their purpose. This conclusion cannot survive even a casual comparative survey. A number of developing countries, Mexico, Pakistan, and Liberia, for example, have established separation-of-powers or presidential systems in which the President is the dominant power and the legislature has no effective role in forming policy. Even in the United States, for that matter, a great number of people besides Congressmen are disquieted by the growth of Presidential power, especially in foreign affairs, and question whether Congress still is capable of calling the President to account.

Given the evidence that neither the separation-of-powers organization nor parliamentary institutions has been effective in stanching the flow of power from the legislature to the executive, one might argue that a hybrid form combining the best features of the two types would provide an effective compress, thus demonstrating that institutional arrangements are, in fact, fundamentally important. The Fifth French Republic does little, however, to credit this belief. Its constitution provides for a President possessing significant powers who is elected independently of the legislature for a fixed term, while also creating a Council of Ministers which must retain majority support in the legislature to remain in office. The power of the French executive in this system is immense not only compared with what it had been under the Third and Fourth Republics, but also with that of other executives. President de Gaulle dominates the French policy-making process more pervasively than any peacetime American President, perhaps including even George Washington, ever dominated the American governmental system.

The striking change in executive power from the Fourth to the Fifth Republic suggests the hypothesis that although institutional arrangements may not be able to prevent executive power from expanding, perhaps they can be influential in greatly accelerating the shift in power from the legislature to the executive. But the evidence is not sufficient to warrant accepting this view. Most experts on French politics are convinced that the way in which the institutions of the Fifth Republic function depends to a very great extent upon the personality of President de Gaulle—so much so, that some of them refer to the Fifth Republic as the de Gaulle Republic. They expect these institutions to operate differently when he is no longer President. The Premier might be more powerful than the President, for example, were someone other than de Gaulle President and certainly would be more powerful had de Gaulle chosen to occupy that office rather than be President. As to why he chose the latter office, he had apparently been influenced by France's previous political experience to conceive of the Premier's role as requiring active involvement in partisan politics in constantly patching together a supporting coalition in the legislature. This de Gaulle disdained to do. He preferred instead to hold an office which he regarded as being above the trivial political squabbles of the legislature and free to deal with matters of national prestige. Thus even in the case of a new political system with offices virtually freshly minted, role expectations rather than institutional provisions were most significant, for so far as the constitutional provisions were concerned the power balance between the office of President and Premier was unclear.

Another example of faith in the efficacy of institutional reform is the belief widely held in Britain by politicians, political journalists, and academics alike that replacing the existing ad hoc legislative committees with permanent specialist committees would significantly strengthen Parliament and increase its ability to call the executive to account. To many Americans this is a curious remedy. The existence of Foreign Affairs and Foreign Relations Committees does not seem to have convinced many Congressmen that the Congress can adequately control the President's direction of American foreign policy, especially in Southeast Asia. In fact, an expert international relations specialist, Hans Morgenthau, has argued to the contrary that if the United States were a parliamentary system, popular discontent with the war in Vietnam would have forced President Johnson out of office in 1966 or 1967—thus contending that control over the executive is greater in Britain than it is in the United States despite the presence of specialist committees in the American Congress and the absence of them in the British Parliament.

While the impact of specialist committees may be limited in the United States by the separation-of-powers system, it is not in Germany, which like Britain has a parliamentary system. Granted that specialist committees in the German Bundestag affect legislation more than do floor debates, it is far from certain that the Bundestag can exert a greater check upon the executive in Germany than the House of Commons can upon the British executive. Nor have permanent subject-matter committees in the French parliament enjoyed any marked success in calling President de Gaulle to account.

Knowing that he may have to justify a policy to informed critics may deter an official to some extent from initiating ill-considered programs and acting arbitrarily. Ultimately, however, the power to say no is what is crucial. Congress's ability to reject Presidential proposals gives the specialist committees whatever sting they possess; if they are unsatisfied, the President may not get what he wants. Whether a legislature employs such power against an executive does depend in part upon institutional arrangements. Separation of powers permits different parties simultaneously to control the executive and the legislature—a result normally impossible in parliamentary systems—and thus would seem to be more likely to encourage legislative-executive clashes.

A structural factor, party cohesion, affects the relationship much more significantly, however. Do legislators belonging to the same party tend to vote in a group according to the instructions of their party leaders or do some of them vote one way and others another? If the latter, then whether a country's political system is parliamentary or separation of powers matters little, for the Government will succeed in having its legislative proposals enacted no more frequently in the one than in the other. True, in the separation-of-powers system the executive remains in office for a fixed term. If an executive is prevented from governing, however, if he cannot obtain legislative approval for his policies, then remaining in office is mere flagpole sitting.

How cohesive parties affect legislative-executive relations depends in part on the number of parties able to win parliamentary seats. If several parties are successful and will not cooperate with each other, the executive will probably lack a stable legislative majority even though each party is cohesive. However, when parties are sufficiently willing to work together so that the extive enjoys the continuing support of a firm majority composed of however many parties, or one party has a majority of the legislative seats, the parliamentary system functions differently from the separation of powers only if the same party or party grouping fails to win both the executive and legislative elections. For when a cohesive party controls both the executive and legislative bodies, the executive's policies are enacted just as smoothly in the separation-of-powers system as in the parliamentary system.

The point is, then, that Congress can control the President to some extent, not so much because of the separation-of-powers system but because Congressmen are willing to vote against the wishes of the President even though they belong to the same party—because party cohesion is relatively low.[2] Unless British legislators are prepared to vote against the Cabinet almost as a matter of course; unless, that is, British parties become markedly less cohesive than they have been for most of this century, creating specialist committees hardly would be likely to strengthen parliamentary control of the executive: Parliament would lack the sanction which makes these committees effective. Yet British students of Parliament persist in the conviction that this institutional reform is the panacea for the malaise which their country's legislature causes them.

These matters are also relevant to the debate as to whether some institutions are more effective and efficient than others. Some students of American politics have argued that the British Parliament satisfies these criteria more fully than does the American Congress. As one argument for this viewpoint, they cite occasions on which Parliament has cut taxes to stimulate the British economy, allowed sufficient time for this action to be effective, and then raised taxes to prevent excessive inflation, all while Congress is still pondering whether the American economy needs a tax cut. Leaving unchallenged the questionable logic of equating despatch with efficiency, this argument rests not on institutional differences, but rather on differences in party cohesion. If American parties were as cohesive and disciplined as British, tax cuts would speed through the Congress also. On the other hand, such cohesion could deadlock the government so severely that it would produce a major constitutional crisis if the party winning the Presidency should fail to control the Congress too, as happened during most of Eisenhower's two terms. That the Democratic legislative leaders, Sam Rayburn and Lyndon Johnson, decided to be amenable to Eisenhower's proposals, rather than intransigent, was of the greatest importance. Even though Congressional Democrats were not as cohesive as British parliamentary parties, they were sufficiently disciplined so that Johnson and Rayburn could have blocked action on a number of programs.

Institutional arrangements, then, should not be dismissed as irrelevant to the political process. They are part of the environment, the context, within which political activity occurs, just as are other factors such as a country's natural resources, educational level, and geographical location. These factors obviously affect the political process; they may impose some broad limits or requisites on it. Yet other factors influence more significantly the actual performance of the political process within those bounds. A Triumph TR-3 can go more than 100 miles an hour; when driven by a little old lady, however, it is unlikely to move even half that fast.

Those who believe in the utility of constitutional tinkering are not so naive as to argue that institutional arrangements alone can determine how a political system operates. They recognize that other factors may affect its performance. But they tend to regard those factors as intervening, almost extraneous, variables which thwart the natural impact of institutional arrangements and render them to some extent ineffective. The danger in this attitude is that it may lead to using these other factors to explain away cases which fail to conform to a hypothesis concerning the effect of a certain institution. Thus a hypothesis may be accepted without adequate evidence, and the other factors, which may be considerably more significant, may not be studied adequately.

Parliamentary Structures' Influence on Parties

Because this chapter emphasizes structures rather than institutions, I will not recount the procedural and organizational arrangements of various political organs throughout the world. Nor will I report which countries have a bicameral parliament and what percentage of those who do give the upper chamber an absolute veto in what percentage of the cases for what type of legislation. Nor, since the variety within each category is so great, will I discuss which countries have parliamentary institutions and which separation of powers or some type of hybrid. Nor will I contrast countries whose courts have the power of judicial review, in the narrow sense of the ability to declare laws unconstitutional, with those which do not, explaining in the process in what special circumstances in each case the power can be exercised. An idea of the futility of such an approach can be seen from the fact that judicial review is more effective, more operative, in the United States, where the power has no basis in the letter of its Constitution, than it is in Italy, whose Constitution specifically provides for it. Some information of the type I have been mentioning is readily available from other sources.[3]

It is more rewarding to examine instead the influence upon parties of various types of parliamentary structures. One of the most striking contrasts between American and British parties is the far greater unity of cohesion the latter demonstrate in their voting in the legislature. On the great majority of votes in the American Congress, many Democrats vote the same way as most Republicans and several Republicans vote with the majority of the Democrats. In Britain, however, only very rarely does a member of one party vote with the members of another party. Members of each party in the House of Commons are told how they must vote by their party leaders and may encounter serious political difficulties if they persist in ignoring these instructions.

Institutionalists have attempted to explain this difference in party behavior by citing the power of the British Prime Minister to dissolve Parliament at any time and call for new elections. They argue that if some legislators who usually support the Prime Minister oppose passage of a bill he favors, he can threaten to call an election, in which they may be defeated. To avoid losing their office, they vote as he instructs them to do. British and French experience is supposed to prove this proposition. The British Prime Minister can call for new elections whenever he desires, and British parties are cohesive.

In Third and Fourth Republic France the executive lacked this powerful weapon to control the legislature and was weak. In arguing from French experience, the institutionalist must concede this argument partially from the beginning, for the problem in France was not a failure of constitutional engineering but a matter of custom and usage. Early in the Third Republic, a French President with monarchical preferences dissolved parliament in an effort to get a cabinet and a legislature more sympathetic to his views. French republicans considered this attempt a virtual coup—a thinly veiled effort to subvert the newly established and still highly fragile parliamentary republic. The power was so discredited, therefore, that French Premiers subsequently did not dare to avail themselves of it, for to have done so would have compromised their republican credentials. Almost eighty years elapsed before a Premier had sufficient courage to use the power. During this time the French executive was usually unable to control parliament effectively.

When this argument—that the ability to dissolve parliament is one of the executive's most powerful means of controlling parliament—is examined more thoroughly, it becomes clear that it glosses over the linkage essential to establish its validity. The threat of a new election can terrorize into line only legislators who might lose their office, which is by no means necessarily all of them. An election may be inconvenient or expensive for a legislator who regularly wins by large majorities, but it can hardly jeopardize his political career. If the threat of dissolution is to be effective, then, the number of legislators holding "safe" seats must be relatively small. No study has ever attempted to estimate the number of "safe" seats in France, and given the frequent changes in the French electoral laws, this may be an impossible task.

In Britain, however (and in the United States, too), studies have shown that the great bulk of the seats are "safe." [4] Except in unusual circumstances, few legislators need fear defeat; they are unlikely to be intimidated by the threat of having to fight an election. In fact, the person most likely to lose if an election is called is the Prime Minister or Premier himself. Enough seats may shift hands from one party to another to remove his Government from office, especially since it is fighting an election at the worst possible time—when riven by schisms which led him to call an election in a disciplinary effort. Thus, most of the legislators are likely to lose little more than the time they must spend in campaigning, while the Prime Minister could lose the status and power of his office and be reduced to just another legislator. The Prime Minister who dissolves Parliament to punish his rebellious followers is much more accurate than the irate parent about to spank his child who says, "This is going to hurt me more than it hurts you."

Since legislators representing "safe" seats need not fear an election, presumably they can afford to be more rebellious. Basic as this point is to the validity of the dissolution power hypothesis, no study has investigated it in a single country, to say nothing of doing so comparatively. The relevant reverse inquiry—are those who break party discipline more likely to represent "safe" seats?—has been examined, but only in Britain. These studies have found that legislators from "safe" seats are less likely to deviate from their party's voting instructions because they are expendable; anyone can retain for the party a seat which it has won repeatedly by large margins.[5] The legislator who was elected by only a few votes more than his opponent cannot be jettisoned so easily, however, for the number of votes his personality attracts may well be the difference between victory and defeat for his party in that seat.

Whether the threat of a new election is sufficiently dreadful, therefore, to deter a legislator from breaking party discipline depends not so much on what he anticipates the voters will do to him as it does on how he expects his party to treat him if he rebels. If party structure is decentralized and the local organization is the legislator's own personal machine, he need not fear reprisals, and an election is no danger. If the party is so centralized that national parliamentary leaders control candidatures throughout the country, however, he could be purged, and a new election would mark the end of his career, provided that most voters were more committed to his party than they were to him personally and did not consider him a martyr. In a single-member, simple-plurality electoral system, like that used in the United States and Great Britain, his party would refuse to renominate him, while in a proportional-representation system, like that used in Italy and Fourth Republic France, his name could simply be moved from the top of the list of candidates for his constituency to the bottom, for the person at the head of a major party's list is virtually assured of being elected, while the one at the bottom of a full list of candidates has no chance of winning.

Still a third possibility is that although the party is not highly centralized concerning matters of candidature, neither does the legislator control his local party organization. In this case a legislator from a "safe" seat who voted against the national leaders of his party might not be purged if his local party supporters agreed with his behavior. Contrary to widespread belief, the third possibility is much closer to the actual situation prevailing in Britain than is the second.[6] Unfortunately, thorough studies of the party procedures for selecting candidates in other countries have not been published, so there is no way of knowing whether legislators who break party discipline are purged either by orders of the national leaders or preferences of the local members, and whether large majorities make legislators more cautious about alienating their party, as is the case in Britain.

The dissolution hypothesis illustrates well the weakness of most institutional generalizations. The case for its acceptance rests on some unwarranted logical assumptions, the reverse of which are just as sensible, and a few selected examples. Evidence concerning some links of the argument crucial to confident acceptance of the hypothesis is lacking. The fact that the institution being studied can be found in diametrically opposed situations, suggesting that other factors may be more significant variables, is glossed over. These contrasting situations are charged to special extenuating circumstances—despite the fact that one may finally have more exceptions to the rule than examples of it and in some instances is reduced to basing a hypothesis supposed to be generally valid upon a single instance, since all the other cases do not quite fit.

In reacting against such faulty explanations, some political scientists went to the opposite extreme, ignoring not only institutions but political structures as well, and stressing instead social and environmental factors. Regarding the question at hand— British parliamentary party cohesion, for example—they would argue that Britain is a small, homogeneous country with distinct social classes and a high level of class voting, which helps to encourage the development of parties which are more ideologically oriented, or programmatic, and well organized on a mass basis; that is, they have formal dues-paying membership open to everyone and do not function just as electoral machines, but continue to operate and discuss policy between elections.

Comparing Canadian and American parties, however, questions the explanatory power of these factors.[7] Both Canada and the United States are large, diversified, and federal, not only legally, but in the effective distribution of power. Neither country has mass, programmatic parties nor a sharply stratified class system. Presumably, then, their parties should behave similarly in the legislature. Yet Canadian parties, like British parties, are disciplined and cohesive, while American parties are not. American parties operate in the context of a separation-of-powers system; Canadian parties in a British-type parliamentary system. A functional requisite of the latter system is that the great bulk of legislators in all but the most exceptional cases vote as their leaders instruct them to. Thus this structural factor, which the

Canadian political system shares with the British, overcomes the environmental similarities between Canada and the United States to produce different behavior by legislators in these two countries.

This argument should not be mistaken as an instance of neo-institutionalism. The effective factor is structural. The focus is upon the influence of the roles and values associated with a particular legal institution, which although associated with it are not provided for in law and thus are a broader concern. A parliamentary system as a legal institution does not produce cohesive, disciplined parliamentary parties. It certainly did not do so in Third and Fourth Republic France, nor, to a very great extent, has it in Fifth Republic France, for example.

Although France, Canada, and Britain all have parliamentary institutions, the French parliamentary structure differs sharply from the other two, which closely resemble each other. That is, Canadian and British political culture are similar, and the roles associated with the parliamentary system and performed by political actors in these two countries are similar, and these cultures and roles contrast with those in France. This contrast emerges clearly from Nathan Leites' attempt to specify the "rules of the game" in Fourth Republic France. Judged by their behavior, French legislators seemed to be acting in accord with several implicit principles, among which were: (1) escape responsibility at all costs, (2) never interpret someone's support for a proposal as indicating that he has accepted it, (3) postpone decisions as long as possible, (4) permit the Government to act only when catastrophe is imminent.[8] These are not the "rules of the game" in Britain. For example, one of the basic aims of the British system is to fix responsibility.

Similarly, the Canadian parliamentary structure encourages legislators to behave in ways which tend not to be regarded as suitable in the American separation-of-powers system.[9] An American Congressman who always voted with his party would risk being dismissed as little more than a party hack. Independence is a trait American political culture values in legislators and virtually requires when necessary to express the views of the legislator's constituents. The Southern Congressman who tells voters that he supported civil rights legislation in Congress because his party leaders instructed him to do so will not be hailed for his party loyalty; rather, he will be defeated for his failure to represent properly the desires of his district. The majority of Canadian legislators, in contrast, feel that rejecting their leaders' voting instructions and breaking party discipline undermines the viability of either their party or the parliamentary system. Parties are more cohesive in the Canadian parliament than the American Congress, but not because Canadian legislators are more afraid than American Congressmen that they will be punished if they break party discipline. Even counting those Canadian legislators who believe that voting as their leaders tell them to is both to their own and their party's advantage, only about a quarter of them mention self-interest as a reason for maintaining party cohesion. Furthermore, about half of Canadian legislators know of no sanction which could be applied to them for breaking the parliamentary "rules of the game." The role appropriate for a legislator in Canada, the way he is expected to behave, simply differs from that which is fitting in the United States; Canada possesses a British parliamentary structure, while the United States does not.

The same argument can be applied to Australia, which, like Canada, when judged on the basis of its varied environment and its federal system of government, would be expected to have political parties no more cohesive than those of the United States. While party schisms have been common, especially in the Australian Labor party, cross-voting is not as prevalent in the Australian parliament as in the American Congress. In this case the roles of British parliamentary structure relevant to legislative cohesion are reinforced by Australians' tendency to emphasize collective efforts rather than individual enterprise. Limited rich soil and a hostile and undependable climate produced a rugged collectivist rather than a rugged individualist on the Australian frontier. The resultant feelings of "mateship" or solidarity have helped to encourage highly disciplined political parties in Australia.

If parliamentary parties in Britain, Canada, and Australia were to become as undisciplined in their legislative voting as American Congressional parties are, they would conflict sharply with established British political values and procedures. They would be rejecting their designated roles. This, of course, could occur; structural analysis does not require positing a fossilized political system. But it would be an event of major significance and would test the political system's adaptability—its ability to incorporate new roles without disrupting the system.

Australia provides a good example of how political practice may not fully satisfy the demands of a particular political structure. The Leader of the Australian Labor party is controlled more closely by the party's legislators than is true in the British Labour party, and the governing organs of the extraparliamentary part of the party—the Conference and the Executive—help to a greater extent than in Britain to determine party policy. The difference is one of degree, for the Leader is pre-eminent and the extraparliamentary organs do not instruct the party's legislators how they must vote on specific bills. Furthermore, when Labor is in power, the cabinet normally is the chief policy maker, with the Conference and Executive acquiescing in its decisions. Nonetheless, actual behavior does depart farther in Australia than in Britain from those roles which McKenzie has explained are structurally requisite for the British parliamentary system.[10] The strength of the British parliamentary structure—the fact that this system does make certain demands upon political actors—is evident from the electoral mileage the Liberal party has obtained from assailing the Australian Labor party's organizational structure. So telling were its attacks in 1963 on Labor's "36 faceless men"—the members of the party Conference, none of whom were in the national parliament—that Labor was forced to reform its party organization to involve the parliamentary leaders directly in the Conference's deliberations.

In other types of parliamentary structures, the demands for

parliamentary party autonomy are weak or nonexistent. Italy has parliamentary institutions, but lacks a British parliamentary structure. The accepted practice there is for extraparliamentary organs to tell a party's legislators how they are to behave. This has been carried even to the extent of the extraparliamentary party requiring a Premier to resign, although he still retained the support of a majority in parliament, as the executive of the Christian Democratic party did to Premier Segni in 1960.

The extreme form of extraparliamentary domination of a party's legislators occurs in communist parties. The top extraparliamentary organ decides what the party's policy and strategy will be and all members, including any who have been elected to parliament, must implement these orders unquestionably. Clearly, the communists in any country care little for the demands of a British parliamentary structure, if it exists there, and do not intend to abide by the rules of the parliamentary game if it is inconvenient to do so.

Mention of the communists' attitude should help to clarify further what it means to say that a system or structure makes certain demands. No one is compelled to grant these demands; one can choose to break the "rules of the game," can refuse to fill the role appropriate to his position in a particular structure. To do so, however, is to challenge the existing structure at least to some extent. As long as the instances of this are relatively few and limited, they cause little trouble. If they grow, they threaten the system. For the rules and roles help to make behavior more predictable; they help to satisfy the system's intrinsic demands. Thus, they enable the existing structures to function efficiently, rationally, while maintaining their stability.

In emphasizing the effect of political structures upon the political process, I do not intend to dismiss environment. Structure and environment do interact. The fact that Canada is much more diversified socially and geographically than Britain does alter the impact of the parliamentary system. Combining the British parliamentary system's demand for legislative party cohesion with Canada's diversity results in a multiparty system; unlike the situation in more homogeneous Britain, two major parties are much less successful in embracing all the varied views which exist in Canada and still remaining united.

The Misleading Federal-Unitary Dichotomy

Another institutional arrangement widely thought even now to influence greatly a country's political process is the way in which powers are allocated between the national and subnational governments, whether a country has federal or unitary institutions. This dichotomy is regarded as so fundamental that it is thought desirable to study as a special group of nations having federal institutions. It is assumed that these nations' political processes resemble each other more than they do those of countries' distributing power between national and subnational governments differently. Stressing a federal-unitary dichotomy is not, however, a very fruitful approach to political analysis; it yields few insightful hypotheses.

The immediate problem encountered by one who stresses the importance of this institutional arrangement is to decide which countries fall in which category. For political scientists do not agree on the essential criteria of a federal system, nor on which countries possess the criteria which have been proposed. (It is as though an entomologist could not distinguish between a butterfly and a moth.) William Riker, for example, feels that eighteen nations qualify for the label "federal," while Banks and Textor's *A Cross-Polity Survey* lists fifteen nations as either "effective" or "limited" federal systems and another six as being either "formal or limited formal federal structure[s]." The work by K. C. Wheare, which was the standard study of federalism for many years, approaches the subject much more legalistically and restricts the number of federal systems to Australia, Canada, Switzerland, and the United States, while conceding that only another three to five nations may be "quasi—federal." [11]

Even determining which countries can be considered federal systems is little aid to further study. The sixteen countries which both Riker and Banks and Textor consider federal at least to some extent are so diversified that they seem to have nothing in common.* Considered as a group, they suggest few hypotheses.

Even rather superficial generalizations about federalism's impact upon other institutions cannot survive cursory examination. Logically one would expect a federal country to have a bicameral legislature; in addition to a chamber representing the people, another chamber would be necessary to express the interests of the constituent units of the federal system. To a considerable extent this expectation is correct; of these sixteen federal systems only Pakistan and, perhaps, Yugoslavia, do not have a bicameral system. This fact alone, however, reveals little about federalism, for it says nothing about the powers of the chamber in which the constituent units are represented. If this chamber is only an advisory body, it hardly could defend the interests of the constituent units, and the legislature might just as well be unicameral. Yet in few of these federal systems does the power of the constituent units' chamber equal that of the other house; typically the former body is regarded as secondary or inferior. Even in two of the only four countries which meet Wheare's stringent definition of federalism the chamber representing the constituent units is the weaker house. The Australian Senate, even though it is popularly elected, and the Canadian Senate, which is appointive, lack some of the power and prestige of their legislative counterparts, most significantly the ability to vote the cabinet out of office.

Merely correlating the existence of two legislative houses with federal institutions also fails to consider how legislators are selected, even though the role of the constituent unit chamber may turn on what method is employed. While the United States Senate is as powerful as the House of Representatives, it does not protect the interests of the states as states. Before the Seventeenth Amendment to the United States Constitution providing

---

* These sixteen are Argentina, Australia, Austria, Brazil, Canada, Germany, India, Malaysia, Mexico, Nigeria, Pakistan, Switzerland, the United States, the USSR, Venezuela, and Yugoslavia.

for direct election of Senators was ratified in 1913, Senators were chosen by state legislatures and could be said to some extent to represent the states as constituent units. Now that Senators are responsible to the voters just as Congressmen are—the only difference being the size of the constituency—this is no longer true. In this regard Germany, which Wheare considers to be only a "quasi—federal" system, is more federal than the United States, since the members of its *Bundesrat* are delegates chosen by the *Land* (state) cabinets and vote as instructed by them.

If distinguishing between federal and unitary systems merely failed to suggest fruitful hypotheses for further research, it would be failure enough; unfortunately, however, classifying countries on this basis obscures relations which might profitably be investigated. Some political systems are obviously more centralized than others; in some, more decisions of greater importance are made by the national government than by the subnational governments. Whether the one situation or the other prevails does not seem to have much to do with whether a country has federal institutions. Northern Ireland, for example, possesses considerable autonomy to deal with its own affairs through its own legislature, cabinet, and courts, although it is part of the United Kingdom of Great Britain and Northern Ireland. True, some of the laws passed by Parliament in London, to which Northern Ireland sends representatives, apply in Northern Ireland, but some of the laws passed by the American Congress apply, for example, in Mississippi.

Supposedly, the difference is that the matters about which Mississippi can make authoritative decisions, having been established by the United States Constitution, cannot be changed by the national government alone; the national government cannot reduce the powers of a state government except in the valid exercise of the powers given to the national government by the Constitution. The powers of the government of Northern Ireland, however, were granted it by Parliament. Therefore, Parliament can withdraw any or all of them any time it chooses to do so. The law permits this, but politically it is impossible. In reality

Parliament cannot rescind its grant of power. Northern Ireland would be no more autonomous if it were part of a federal system.

Yet the United Kingdom is labeled a unitary government and as such is classified with France, a country which is highly centralized through the prefect system. Prefects are national agents in charge of all governmental services in a particular area, regardless of whether some of these are paid for by local government, whose extensive powers include removal from office of some local officials whom prefects feel are not discharging their duties properly. Such a system would be unthinkable in Northern Ireland. Classifying the United Kingdom with the United States as relatively decentralized systems, in contrast to the highly centralized French system, is more likely to yield informative research findings than is grouping the United Kingdom and France together as having unitary institutions in contrast to countries with federal institutions, like the United States.

More important than institutional arrangements, then, is the peoples' attitude toward central control, their role expectations —whether they feel it is fitting that most decisions be made by the national government or subnational governments. Requiring all schools in the United States to desegregate racially is difficult not so much because the country has federal institutions, but because Americans strongly believe that the schools should be controlled locally—even within a single state the educational system is typically decentralized—and often are racially prejudiced. If these attitudes did not exist, implementing the Supreme Court's desegregation decision would not cause great difficulty. Compliance would be as widespread as in a unitary system.

While politics in Britain is not as regionally diverse as in the United States, Americans have overemphasized Britain's homogeneity. Economic, religious, cultural, and even, to some extent, language differences separate Britain into distinct regions whose interests do not always coincide. Furthermore, Britain has a strong tradition of active local government. Thus, although a national Department of Education and Science has ultimate power in some regards over the state-supported school system, many important decisions about the schools are made by the local educational authorities. National control of the schools is tighter than in the United States, but not nearly as stringent as in France. Once again Britain seems to resemble the United States more than it does France, a fact which the federal-unitary dichotomy tends to obscure.

Federalism sometimes is cited as one of the factors helping to maintain a two-party system in the United States. It supposedly permits a party which persistently loses national elections to retire to state bailiwicks, which have resisted the national trend to the opposing party, to recuperate for further electoral challenges of the nationally dominant party.

Regardless of whether this has occurred in the United States (the argument has not been firmly established), it has not been true in Canada. Most party strongholds in Canadian provincial politics are preserves of the party which has dominated national politics in Canada for most of this century—the Liberals.[12] The Canadian evidence as readily warrants the opposite conclusion —that a federal system facilitates a multiparty system by establishing regional centers of governmental power, which a minor national party has a better chance of controlling, if it can concentrate its support, than it does the national government. In such areas, at least, the minor party does not seem irrelevant, since it actually governs. But not only has the party system not developed in this way under the American federal system; the evidence from Australia and Germany does not seem to support this hypothesis. Although neither of these federal countries has a two-party system, third parties in national politics are, at best, no more than junior partners in coalitions at the constituent-unit level. Thus, while they do draw more support in some areas than in others, the federal units as such do not offer them a bastion from which they can fight national elections.

Federalism may, however, have some effect on the way power is distributed within parties. As we have already seen, the mass party organization of the Labor party in Australia has somewhat greater influence upon party policy than is true of mass parties in Britain. This influence seems to be checked in part by the federal system, which, even in a country where the constituent units do not represent very significant diversity, is a serious impediment to any extraparliamentary organ exercising control over legislators.[13] The problem is that no satisfactory method has been devised for representing in the national body which is to control the legislators the various state parties, which naturally exist in a federal system to contest elections at the constituent-unit level. If power is distributed equally among the state parties, the large parties are dissatisfied; if power varies with population or party membership, the small parties are unhappy. To avoid perpetual sectional conflict in the party, control of the legislators must be left primarily to the party leaders in the legislature, who are allowed a relatively free hand. But since this situation is a functional requisite of the British parliamentary system, it cannot be attributed to the impact of federalism alone. Federalism may have some influence; once again, however, its effect is limited.

Varieties of Bureaucratic Structures

Having discussed legislatures and parliamentary parties from a structural, rather than an institutional, perspective, I now wish to do the same for bureaucracies. Rather than summarize the conditions of service, the retirement benefits, the means of discipline, and other such detailed aspects of civil services in a number of countries, I will discuss how bureaucratic structures vary and to what these variations are related.[14]

While a more elaborate taxonomy might be desirable for some purposes, several significant contrasts can be discovered by thinking of bureaucracies as running the spectrum from nascent to full maturity and comparing the ideal types or models to be found at each end of this spectrum. For ease of reference I will label these two models professionalized and nonprofessionalized.

The role of the professionalized bureaucracy is to implement the policies upon which other structures have decided. While it may be involved in the process of determining authoritative policies, it does not dominate that process. Controlled effectively by other structures, its autonomy is limited. Thus, it is largely restricted to its well-defined and relatively narrow primary function of executing policy. It performs other functions, such as expressing interests, only adventitiously; discharging these is the main concern of other structures.

The professionalized bureaucracy is also specialized in another regard; it is characterized by a large number of agencies, each of which deals with a very restricted range of issues and is staffed by highly trained experts. From this feature it follows that the professionalized bureaucracy recruits its personnel on the basis of their abilities and sends them through a rather lengthy training program. This program not only helps to fit them for their specialized work, but also helps to inculcate the values of the bureaucracy—it begins to "professionalize" them. Professionalized bureaucrats regard government service as a career in the same way a doctor or a lawyer would regard his work as a profession. They are concerned to know and conform to the procedures, the rules of behavior, which their colleagues deem correct. They have a sense of belonging to a group, which is in some ways distinct from other occupations. They take pride in doing their work well and feel that if they perform badly, it will reflect upon their colleagues and their occupation in general; conversely, they regard anything detrimental to their profession as reflecting upon them personally.

In contrast to this, the nonprofessionalized bureaucracy is multifunctional to a much greater extent. It is intimately involved in the making of policy and is likely to dominate this process; it is one of the principal channels for expressing and focusing demands for authoritative action. Largely autonomous, it is controlled little by other structures. What control exists is exerted by the leading executives or a dominant political party, rarely by parliamentary structures. The agencies of nonprofessionalized bureaucracies are little specialized; nor are their staffs, given a shortage of skilled manpower, highly trained to deal with specific tasks. Recruitment is not by merit. While the nonprofessionalized bureaucrat may feel that he derives considerable prestige from holding a government job, he does not regard his work as a profession requiring certain types of behavior, nor does he sense a community of interest with others performing similar work. Finally, the nonprofessionalized bureaucracy is not concerned only, or even primarily, to administer government business effectively; it helps achieve other goals such as furthering personal social mobility and serving as an employment agency to help reduce the level of unemployment.

The extent to which a particular country's bureaucracy corresponds to one or the other of these two models is related in part to its level of economic development. Bureaucracies in countries whose economies are highly advanced are likely to be professionalized, while those in countries with rudimentary technologies are not. Thus bureaucracies are relatively professionalized in most of Western Europe and North America and relatively nonprofessionalized in Asia and Africa. A country like Japan, whose economy has developed rapidly in the last decade and which to some extent is still modernizing, falls between these two groups.

Factors other than economic development also significantly affect bureaucratic structures, as indicated by the numerous ways in which countries at one end or the other of the spectrum differ from each other. In France and Germany people regard the bureaucrat as an official—one who personally embodies the state's sovereignty. This view, plus the knowledge that the bureaucrat is highly educated and has had to pass rigorous examinations to attain his position, helps to encourage Germans to defer to the bureaucrat and to allow him a relatively active role in forming policy. The French, in keeping with their traditional suspicion of governmental authority, have tended to ridicule the bureaucrat, rather than defer to him. Nonetheless, the French, like the Germans, think of the bureaucrat as an official rather than as a public servant. Thus, although they may oppose him or refuse to cooperate with him, they recognize that it is his role to give them orders rather than be instructed by them. Given this status, it is fitting in France also that the bureaucrat be involved to a considerable extent in making authoritative decisions. Furthermore, a multiparty system combined with low cohesion in some parties made the French executive short-lived and relatively weak during most of the Third and Fourth Republics. In some instances the French bureaucracy had to make policy by default, for the political executive was unable to perform this function adequately. While, then, the French and German bureaucracies have been professionalized, specialized, and hierarchically structured for many years, bureaucrats in these countries have not abstained from participating actively in the process of forming authoritative policy and, particularly in France, have not always been controlled effectively by other political structures.

Britons and Americans tend not only to regard the government expert as an inexperienced know-it-all given to impractical schemes, but also not to regard him as a symbol of governmental authority. They conceive of him as a public servant, not an official. Therefore, he, rather than they, should be obsequious. This attitude is related in part to the prevalence of the idea, especially in the United States, that government is everybody's business, that everyone should participate in some phase of the political process. Significant decisions should not be left to bureaucrats. Also relevant to the relatively low status of the American bureaucrat is the continued acceptance of the Jacksonian dictum that anyone who can read, write, and cipher is fit for government service.

Although the British never went quite this far, they have long been convinced that in most endeavors, including government service, the gifted amateur is preferable to the expert. A classical education—the ability to read Homer in the original—is sufficient to make one the master of men and all imaginable situations and is, therefore, not only adequate but highly appropriate training for government service. A management specialist is regarded as a mere technician who lacks the agility of mind essential for dealing with extraordinary circumstances. Thus in these nations the bureaucracy has not been as multifunctional as in France and Germany; while it has not been confined solely to executing the decisions made by other structures, this has been its primary purpose. Furthermore, bureaucrats have not been professionalized as long or to the same extent as in France and Germany, although this is less true in Britain than in the United States and hardly true at all in the case of the British Foreign Service. Nonetheless, these countries' bureaucracies are clearly closer to the professionalized than to the nonprofessionalized end of the spectrum. They do recruit their personnel on merit; they are organized into specialized agencies hierarchically related to each other, as are the staff themselves; they do not serve such extraneous purposes as providing a means of reducing unemployment; they are the agents for implementing the policies of the decision makers.

Another economically developed nation, the Soviet Union, adds further variety to forms of professionalized bureaucracies. Its bureaucracy is even less autonomous than that of Britain or the United States. The Communist Party, while separate from the bureaucracy, is connected closely with it at a number of points to insure that the party's wishes will not be thwarted. Some of the methods of control employed by the party, however, tend to prevent the bureaucracy from coinciding with the model professionalized bureaucracy. Welfare agencies are not as hierarchically organized as they could be because overlapping chains of command multiply the number of agencies capable of checking on administrative performance. Thus, various officials compete with each other's authority and have a vested interest in keeping each other under surveillance. Employing mutual suspicion as a means of control clearly tends to hinder the growth of feelings of a community of interest necessary for a fully professionalized bureaucracy. Another negative result is that conflicting lines of command prevent an agency from functioning at top efficiency. Therefore, the Russians have been forced to abandon this type of administrative organization in areas like industry and foreign trade, where the demands of modernizing their nation's economy require the most efficient performance possible. To this extent the bureaucrats gain some autonomy and are able to exert some influence on the policy-making process. The party remains in control of the bureaucracy, however, because it provides the arena within which differences over policy are fought out. Kosygin may express the views of the industrial bureaucrats as contrasted with Brezhnev, the leader of the party bureaucrats, but they resolve their disagreements within the party's leading organ. This process, then, cannot correctly be termed a struggle between the party and the bureaucracy. Rather, it is a question of whose views will win the party's support.

The Russian bureaucracy lacks the hierarchical structure of the full professionalized bureaucracy for a further reason. The penalty for mistakes tends to be so severe in the Soviet Union that administrators are excessively cautious. Thus many decisions which should have been made at a subordinate level are sent higher up the chain of command in an effort to avoid any responsibility for potential failures.

Thus France, Germany, Britain, the United States, and the Soviet Union are all at the high end of the bureaucratic development spectrum as you would expect, given their level of economic development. Yet each fails in some ways to conform exactly to the ideal type or model of the most fully developed bureaucracy. I have argued that this is evidence of the important impact upon bureaucratic structures of popular attitudes, or, to use a term I discussed earlier, political culture. Factors such as political culture and level of economic development mold bureaucratic structures into their actual form; the institutional arrangements have little effect on this form.

This point emerges clearly from a study of the bureaucracies of non-Western nations. In most cases these bureaucracies are not indigenous structures, but rather are a set of institutions copied from a Western nation. As a result the gap between the institutional form and the operational reality is usually great, since the political culture and level of economic development in the countries where the bureaucratic institutions are to be implanted differ so greatly from the countries from which these institutions were derived.

Of course, the performance of bureaucratic structures varies from one developing country to another, as I have already pointed out it does in several countries with developed economies and political systems. This is true even for countries in the same region with similar colonial experience—former British possessions in Asia, for example. Thus, although they are actively involved in the process of deciding policy, the bureaucracies of India and Malaysia are controlled to some extent by political parties. In part this is true in Ceylon as well; there, however, an active trade union movement encompassing a high percentage of government servants also plays an important role in keeping the bureaucracy accountable, while in Pakistan such checks as are exerted over the bureaucracy emanate from the judiciary.

The question of whether and, if so, by what means bureaucratic structures can be made responsible, touches on one of the most significant contrasts of these structures in developing countries. Where party structures have developed sufficiently to be relatively stable and effective, then, regardless of whether the party system is competitive, dominant-one party, or totalitarian, the autonomy of bureaucratic structures and, hence, their impact upon policy-making, is somewhat restricted. Where party structures are rudimentary, however, bureaucratic autonomy and policy influence are greatest.

In what can be called traditional-autocratic regimes—Ethiopia, for example—those which have modernized their political system little, if any, the bureaucracy is at the service of the ruler and thus, perhaps in some sense might be said to be controlled. Yet it is clearly one of the main sources of advice to the ruler and has considerable impact upon those governmental policies which are not attributable merely to the ruler's whim. Furthermore, the ability of such regimes to survive much longer in the second half of the twentieth century is questionable. They seem prime candidates for future membership in that type of regime which involves an alliance between the civil elite and the military elite—a form which can be labeled a bureaucratic elite system. In these countries (Pakistan and Thailand are examples) the policy power of bureaucratic structures is greatest. No other political or social structures are sufficiently strong to challenge effectively the power of the bureaucratic-military alliance. These systems have developed sufficiently to have destroyed the traditional political and social structures like the tribes or kinship groups, thus eliminating these potential checks on arbitrary government action. They have not evolved, however, to the point of establishing viable parliamentary, party, or political group structures and thus have not produced any new means of calling the bureaucracy to account to replace the old, shattered channels of accountability. Their eventual success in making their bureaucracies responsible depends much more on the growth and viability of their political structures than on the form of their legal institutions.

Thus, emphasizing the study of structures rather than institutions is much more likely to yield significant insights into the political process. While a country's constitutional arrangements have some relevance to its politics, their impact is so limited and uncertain that constitutional tinkering is unlikely to be worthwhile. For, as we have seen, constitutions have not prevented a substantial growth in executive power in the twentieth century regardless of the type of institutions they establish and of the intentions of their framers. Nor do they seem to determine whether a political system is decentralized. The extent to which significant decisions are made at the subnational level varies considerably among federal systems; some nations with unitary institutions permit more subnational autonomy than do nations with federal institutions. Role expectations regarding the level of decision making are more influential than constitutional arrangements. Federal institutions do not seem indigenous to a particular type of political system, nor does their presence seem to produce any significant similarities in the political process.

Similarly, the transplanting of Western political institutions to developing nations has not professionalized their bureaucracies and made them politically responsible. The institutional form has not been able to determine the operational reality. What is missing is vigorous alternative political structures, especially political parties, capable of checking bureaucracy and role expectations restrictive of bureaucratic power. The population's attitude toward bureaucrats and its conception of proper bureaucratic behavior restrict the bureaucracy less in some economically developed democracies than in others. But in these systems other political structures usually are established sufficiently well to be able to counterbalance bureaucratic power. In developing nations, where this typically is not the case, the absence of restrictive role expectations is more serious. This is especially true in non-African systems, where the military is more likely to be a well-developed institution. Like the bureaucracy, it is unlikely to be professionalized fully or restricted by role expectations. Thus an alliance between the bureaucracy and the military results in virtually unchecked government.

Role expectations, or structural considerations, also are more important than the power of dissolution—an institutional arrangement—in explaining parliamentary party cohesion. Most legislators in countries that have British parliamentary structures conceive of their role differently from American Congressmen. They feel that regular, loyal support of their party leaders is fitting behavior.

Of course, the impact of similar structures varies from one environment to another. Cohesive parties are compatible with a two-party system in a country which, like Britain, is fairly homogeneous. However, in a diversified country, like Canada, they help to produce a multiparty system or at least a very significantly modified two-party system. Thus, emphasis on the importance of structural factors in contrast with institutional arrangements should not obscure the significant influence of environment on the political system.

The evidence examined here strongly implies that the great concern in West Germany about revising the electoral law to thwart the NDP is misguided. If a sizable number of Germans really want to support a neo-Nazi party, its strength will grow, regardless of whether the electoral system is revised to the single-member, simple-plurality type. However, the charge against constitutional tinkering is not merely that it is likely to be ineffective; more serious is the danger that it may create a false sense of security. Those who believe in the efficacy of legal solutions may think that a problem is solved once a law is passed, and fail to concern themselves with it any longer. If West Germans seriously believe that all they need is electoral reform, the situation truly is perilous.

Chapter 6

Who Governs?

In this survey of comparative politics, I have considered the impact of environment, especially political culture, on the political process; studied varieties of political change, the gradual and relatively peaceful as well as the sudden and violent; examined the channels through which people communicate with those structures empowered to make decisions binding upon an entire society; and argued that the process of converting demands into authoritative pronouncements is affected much more significantly by structures than by legal institutions.

Since actors are one intrinsic element of the concept of structure, I also have been explaining indirectly who controls the political process. Anyone who votes or writes a letter to a governmental official, anyone who belongs to a political party or an interest group, anyone who in some way participates in politics influences the political process to some extent. Even people who do none of these things affect the political process by whether they generally comply with the laws and whether they do so grudgingly or willingly. National Prohibition was not repealed in the United States because a large number of people wrote their Congressmen in protest, but because it became obvious that the jails were not large enough to hold all those who were making gin in their bathtubs. Also, the profits of bootlegging were making criminal gangs dangerously strong. Widespread disregard of the law was more effective in changing it than a letter-writing campaign would have been.

To suggest that everyone is involved in the political process sounds too much like the democratic rhetoric found in high school civics books. It is like responding to the question, "Who owns the wealth of the United States?" by saying "Everyone who has even a penny in his pocket." Political power, like wealth, is distributed unequally. The sophisticated, perhaps a bit cynical, student wants to know who *really* runs things, who *really* decides, who *really* possesses power riches. Structure includes actors, but who are these key actors, what are they like specifically? What are the characteristics of the political regents I mentioned at the beginning of this book? Who governs?

Characteristics of Political Leaders

People who hold the most prominent governmental positions and are most influential politically are recruited into politics through a variety of structures. In Latin America the church and the military are two of the most important channels for entry, while in the United States those avenues are relatively insignificant. Leaders may have been recruited initially because an acquaintance or relative urged them to become active politically, or (not necessarily intentionally) made politics seem fascinating. Alternatively, the original contacts may have been impersonal—they may have responded to some political structure's general recruitment efforts.

A study of Canadian and American national legislators found that about as many had become interested in politics during childhood as during adult years, while few recalled their interest beginning during adolescence.[1] The great majority of those whose interest started when they were children regarded their families as the decisive influence, while all those who were adults before becoming interested in politics attributed their interest to external events or life circumstances like a war or an economic depression or attending law school. The importance of family influence varied between the two countries; more than half of the Canadian legislators, but only one-third of the American, attributed their political interest to their families' influence. In an earlier discussion of the expression of demands, I noted that family affected political attitudes less in France than in the United States. However, this was only because fewer French fathers than American communicated their partisan preferences to their children; among those who did, the effect of fathers' partisan preferences was as great in one country as the other.

It is not possible to say whether the difference between Canadian and American legislators is due to a similar failure to communicate, or to a national culture difference, or to a contrast between those who attain political leadership positions and those who do not. The authors of the Canadian-American study suggested that politics may be more partisan in Canada than in the United States and that Canadian parties may be more easily distinguishable from each other than are American, and that these facts would help to explain why Canadians would become interested in politics earlier and primarily because of the influence of their families. Not only are these two assumptions about Canadian politics questionable, however, but the French evidence also challenges the argument. Political conflict in France is certainly sharper than in the United States, and yet family has less impact on political attitudes. This is a good example of how broader comparative analysis can help to reject tentative hypotheses, which otherwise might seem acceptable, offered to explain observed differences. Unfortunately, existing research does not suggest any reasons why the Canadian-American difference should have been discovered. I can only note the contrast as an apparent difference in the political recruitment process in Canada and the United States.

Another contrast is that in Canada, more than in the United States, legislators whose fathers had been business or professional men were quite likely to have become interested in politics early in life, while most of those whose fathers held other jobs did not become interested until they were adolescents or adults. While prestige of father's occupation is related to life stage of initial political interest for American legislators, yet even of those who came from a higher-class background, somewhat more became interested in politics as adults than as children. Thus, while the evidence in both countries tends to bear out a relative lack of interest in politics among those of lower-class occupations, on which I will comment more later, the relation is stronger in Canada. Again this is a difference which must go unexplained. Perhaps in a country whose social structure was highly stratified and whose parties divided the population sharply along class lines, political interest might not be related closely to fathers' occupational status. The United States hardly approximates this situation more than does Canada, however.

One final point of interest from this study is that in Canada, and to an even greater extent in the United States, factors other than family influence were instrumental in arousing the initial political interest of national legislators. Important as the family certainly is in shaping political attitudes, other more clearly political structures very frequently play a major role in recruiting political leaders.

To think of leaders as necessarily having been recruited, however, is frequently incorrect. While political parties may have membership drives intermittently, their primary reason for them is usually to secure additional funds and perhaps to find a few people who are willing to devote several hours to addressing envelopes. These drives are not typically very selective, not part of a conscious effort to obtain potential leaders. Civil service systems have established various examining procedures to recruit new personnel. But these serve largely to select the capable from among those who present themselves for employment; they do not tend to be a means of actively seeking new staff. The announcement that a vacancy exists or that exams for admission to the civil service will be given at a specified time is likely to appear only on some out-of-the-way bulletin board and to be obscured by other notices. Frequently those who become political leaders are not so much sought out as they are self-selected. The initiative to participate actively in politics was their own.

This is one reason why some political scientists have argued that political leaders are people who have a "will to power." [2] Various events in their lives have made them psychologically insecure. Displacing private motives on public behavior, they seek positions in which they can dominate others and thus gain some feeling of security. Logical as this argument may sound, research thus far has not succeeded very well in substantiating it. The problem in part is that the concept is difficult to operationalize. How can one ascertain who thirsts to dominate others? Insofar as researchers have decided to accept a particular pattern of answers to a special set of questions as evidence of a personality seeking dominance, they have not found that those who give such answers are especially attracted to politics. Perhaps this is not surprising. All groups must have leaders. Therefore, one who feels a need to dominate others presumably could satisfy it just as well by becoming a priest, a general, or a school principal, instead of a politician.

Efforts to verify the similar hypothesis that political leadership is linked with an authoritarian personality have succeeded even less. Again the problem has been to devise a reliable measure of the concept—one which would permit research results to be replicated by other investigators and one which we could be sure was not being affected by other attitudes or extraneous factors.

While a "will to power" cannot be demonstrated to be associated with political leadership, other psychological characteristics or personal attitudes are related. Political leaders tend to be sociable people, readily able to express themselves, self-disciplined, and self-assured. They believe they are competent to deal with varied and unexpected circumstances and feel politically efficacious. They are psychologically involved in politics, are interested in it and concerned about it, and their attitudes toward politics are positive, not cynical. That the more psychologically involved in politics one is, the more likely he is to be highly active is logical enough in itself; the relation is made even more convincing by the fact that those who are psychologically involved in politics are more likely to feel politically efficacious and, as already noted, those who feel this way are more likely to be highly active.

These relations help to explain in part why certain personal attributes are associated with political leadership. Those who are highly active in politics tend to be better educated men of higher income whose occupations are among the more prestigious and who live in cities. Men are more likely than women to feel both psychologically involved in politics and politically efficacious. They are more likely to receive more political stimuli and the more they do, the more likely they are to participate in politics and the greater the extent of their participation. Others likely to be more highly stimulated politically are those who live in cities, whose status and education are higher, whose attitudes toward politics are positive, and who grew up in homes where politics was frequently discussed. People of higher status and education are less likely to be cynical about politics; thus they not only tend to be more stimulated politically, but they need not overcome the obstacle which political cynicism itself is to a high level of political activity. Their lack of cynicism does not mean they are politically naive; rather, they are knowledgeable and sophisticated about politics. And those who are, are more likely to be highly active in politics. Furthermore, they are more likely to feel psychologically involved in politics and politically efficacious.

Thus, research has revealed a cluster of interrelated, reinforcing variables; some are personal attributes and others are personality characteristics which help to link particular types of people to political leadership. Many of these variables are similar to those noted in a previous chapter which characterize people who participated in politics by expressing demands in some way.

Those who go beyond this level of political activity and become leaders possess these qualities to a higher degree.

This is not to say, of course, that these observations always hold true. These comments are simply statements of general tendencies and marked disproportionalities; you may well know of some contrary cases. The statement that men are more likely than women to be politically involved, for example, does not mean that no woman is politically involved—Margaret Chase Smith and Clare Boothe Luce do not disprove this statement. Rather, this means that the proportion of men who are politically involved is significantly larger than the proportion of women who are.

Some of these leadership characteristics warrant more detailed comment.[3] Education and political activism are related not only in Western, democratic systems. Nazi, Russian and Chinese Communist, and Fascist leaders all tended to have above-average educational attainments. And even in the developing countries, where standards of achievement may differ considerably from those common in Western countries, political leaders tend to come from the better-educated groups. In part, of course, this is because education helps them to master some of the skills useful in politics. In some cases, South Asia for example, it is also attributable to the fact that businessmen, who tend not to be especially well-educated, are not reputed to be very honest. An intellectual is deemed more trustworthy and is accorded greater prestige. It is also relevant that teachers, another more educated group, were not as concentrated in the cities as other potential leadership groups. Being more dispersed throughout the countryside, teachers were often able to develop, through the use of their skills, strong local contacts to serve as a power base. This, combined with their propagandizing and organizational activity in independence movements, won them prominent political positions. Thus when their nations won independence they frequently became the largest occupational group in the legislature. In a selected group of African countries, for example, teachers made up at least 20, and often more than 40 percent, of the legislature.

In some cases, however, the situation seems to be changing. In India and, to an even greater extent in Ceylon, the non-Western, less well-educated politician is becoming more important. Not quite comparable, but relevant, is the discovery that in Japan education does not seem to have the same psychological impact on political attitudes that it has in some other countries. Agreeing with the finding that level of political activity and education are related, the higher the level of education the greater the percentage of people in the United States who desire to have more "influence in community affairs." In Japan this desire does not rise with education. This is evidence neither that educated Japanese do not participate in politics nor that Japanese politicians are poorly educated. Instead, it suggests that in Japan higher education is not as great a motivating factor for more active political involvement as it is in some other political systems.

The relation between an urban background and political leadership seems to be somewhat more of a Western phenomenon. Although in Asia leaders have tended to come from the cities, the previously mentioned rise of the less well-educated politician in Ceylon and India represents a shift in political power from urban to rural areas. And if one focuses on leaders' birthplaces, cities are even less important. Asian political leaders are about as likely to have been born in rural areas as in small towns and either of these much more frequently than in their countries' capital cities, while an overwhelming number of African leaders were born in rural areas. Thus a high proportion of these leaders did not spend their formative years in urban surroundings. Nonetheless, the fact that they probably had a Western education and came from families of civil servants, teachers, and merchants is evidence that they have broken with tradition, at least to some extent.

The occupations of political leaders exhibit some national and regional contrasts. The landed aristocracy retains virtually no political power in Western democracies, while in some developing countries their influence, although waning, is still significant. Curiously, in Turkey and Ceylon the effect of a more competitive party system has been to replace government officials with businessmen and landowners as political leaders. Religious leaders continue to be an important political force, especially at the local level, in some developing countries, another contrast with Western democracies. Like democratic political leaders in many countries, however, the Communist, Fascist, and Nazi leaders tended to come from a middle-class background. They were people who, despite increased social, economic, and cultural mobility in their countries, had not been able to advance themselves politically because the traditional aristocracy continued to dominate politics. Violent ideological movements gave them a road to political power which a superficially democratizing political system had denied. In contrast, both the Communist and non-Communist Chinese political leaders—members of the Kuomintang Central Executive Committee and the Communist Politburo and Central Committee—have tended to be either military men or career party officials, and have tended to come from a much narrower range of occupations than has been the case in Europe or in other Asian political systems.

Even among Western democracies, contrasts exist. In many of these countries lawyers are a sizable group in the parliament; this has not been true in Sweden, however, where farmers and workers have been more predominant. This difference may be due to the party system's tendency to divide the population rather sharply along class lines. In such instances parties may well be disposed to recruit their leaders from these occupational groups they represent, thereby reducing the number of parliamentarians drawn from higher status occupations.

The legal profession has also provided a sizable proportion of cabinet members in the United States, Britain, Germany, and France. Another major source of cabinet members in the United States has been business, while in France journalism has been the other most prevalent occupation. In Britain these three occupations have been approximately equal in providing cabinet members. Even more important than law in Germany has been the civil service. Given the German deference to the civil servant, mentioned in the preceding chapter, this is not particularly surprising.

From this variety of evidence it is clear that political leaders—those who really govern—compose a relatively small proportion of a country's population and are drawn from those who have relatively uncommon characteristics or attributes. The fact that two of these attributes tend to be a higher level of education and higher socio-economic status may seem to suggest that I am saying that all countries, whatever their pretensions to democracy, are in fact ruled by a power elite.

Does an Elite Rule?

A number of studies have answered this question affirmatively, a few on the basis of examining a national political system and more, given the problems of gathering sufficient relevant data at that level, by focusing on a subnational political system. Little of this research has been comparative. National studies have tended to concentrate primarily on a single country.[4] While the community power studies have compared the same city at different times and different American cities with each other, they seldom have compared American cities with cities in other countries.

Two of the exceptions to this procedure present mixed evidence concerning elite rule.[5] A comparison of a British and an American city found that businessmen predominated among the key leaders in the American case but not in the British. This finding was taken as evidence that political power was distributed more broadly in the latter case and that the American city was more nearly governed by an elite. The difference was regarded as being due in part to differing values of occupation prestige from one culture to the other. A study of an American and a Mexican city located opposite, across the border, also found the more elitist power structure in the American city, where the economic and political leadership groups were more closely integrated and overlapped more than they did in the Mexican city. Nonetheless, the researcher did not discover that these two leadership groups were so tightly knit that he could justify terming them a single power elite. Generalizing from such inclusive findings is hardly permissible. About all one can conclude is that, while these studies do little to challenge the belief that elite rule is prevalent in the United States, they fail to suggest that it exists at the local level in other democratic systems, even in the case of a system which is more an aspiring, than a mature, democracy.

The findings on the United States can be challenged, however, because of flaws in the methods used in many community power studies.[6] These studies have tended to assume rather than demonstrate that those who hold major economic positions or have high social status must inevitably wield decisive political power. Thus they have been content merely to identify these people, examine how closely they overlap and interact, and then label them the power elite for that system. They have not focused on particular issues in an effort to discover precisely how and why a specific authoritative decision was made. Instead they have assumed that the already identified power elite must have dominated the decision-making process in every case, or could have done so had it chosen to. The latter qualification makes disproof of the elite rule hypothesis logically impossible. Any empirical evidence which fails to support it can be explained away as an instance in which the elite regarded the issue as too trivial to bother to exercise their power. Thus, supporters of the elite rule hypothesis could maintain that they were correct even if the elite virtually never influenced an authoritative decision.

The proper method of determining who governs is not to ask a number of prominent people, especially businessmen as the asserters of elite rule do, whom they believe the most influential people to be, but to analyze a number of major authoritative decisions to discover who was instrumental in forming them.

While it is not impossible that the same people were most powerful in each case, a finding which would tend to support the elite rule hypothesis, this must be demonstrated, not assumed. Studies which have used a decision-making approach have found that the amount of power certain groups wield depends upon the issue, since the group exercising the most influence varies from one issue to another. These findings are evidence of pluralistic, rather than elite, rule. Although they demonstrate the weakness of the attributional approach to studying power structures and the invalidity of the elite rule hypothesis in some American cities, they do not prove that the power structures of all democracies, at either the national or subnational level, are pluralistic. This will require further research of the type just mentioned.

Even if this research should find that pluralistic power structures are typical of democracies, it would still be true that on any given issue those with the greatest influence would be a relatively small group. As I commented at the beginning of this book, a complex enterprise cannot be managed by all of its members. Some will be leaders and some followers; some will have considerable influence over the action the structure takes and others will not. Those who govern will always be regents even though their identity may change from one issue to another. Furthermore, even though the regents are not always the same people, it is unlikely that everyone will have a turn at being regent. Some, those having the characteristics and attributes discussed earlier, are more likely to attain this position than others. If democracies are not subject to elite rule, perhaps they are to elites' rule.

This prospect, reinforced by the finding that even political parties which profess strong commitment to democratic values are themselves oligarchic in their internal operating procedures, has led Maurice Duverger to argue that we should reject an unattainable and artificial eighteenth-century conception of democracy and seek instead a "true democracy," one in which there is not only "real liberty" and social justice for all, but also one in which representation was restored to its "true" meaning.[7] This system would be: "Government of the people *by an elite sprung from the people.*" If only the regents would mirror exactly the attributes of the citizens, they would truly represent them and, therefore, true democracy, not some lawyer's or philosopher's abstraction, would be attained.

Appealing as this argument may sound, it is deficient in several ways. First, what attributes of the population are the regents to reflect? Economic class alone is hardly sufficient, unless one adopts the Marxist position that economic relations are the foundation upon which the entire superstructure of society depends. One's political values and policy desires are influenced as well by his religion, his race, the region of the country in which he lives, and his education, to mention only a few factors. How many of the virtually endless personal attributes need to be represented? And is it sufficient that the regents simply mirror the gross figures for each attribute selected—40 percent of the population is Catholic so 40 percent of the regents must be, 90 percent are white so 90 percent of the regents must be, disregarding how many of them are Catholic also? Or must they represent the intersection of a number of attributes—5 percent of the population are Southern, white, Catholic workers, etc., so 5 percent of the regents must be also? If the number of attributes to be represented is large, the procedure becomes almost hopelessly complex and inoperable.

Secondly, why should it be assumed that one cannot empathize fully with and zealously defend the interests of one whose background differs from his own? Substantiating this belief would be difficult even for a Communist, were he objective about it, for neither Marx nor Lenin came from a proletarian background, yet they are supposed to have had the workers' interest at heart. In the United States during the 1930s few businessmen believed that Franklin Roosevelt was defending the interests of the wealthy class to which he belonged. Specific instances of advocates of social justice being drawn from the more fortunate groups in society could be compounded. "True" representation is unnecessary.

Furthermore, it may be ineffective. As the previous paragraph and the findings of decision-making community power structure studies imply, the mere fact that a number of people share similar background attributes or characteristics is no proof that they have an identity of interests or desires. Some American workers vote Republican and some Democratic; some British workers vote Labour and some Conservative; some Negroes advocate Black Power, some seek social equality in cooperation with whites, some are Uncle Toms.

The trade union movement, both industrial and political, in a number of democracies has long been haunted by the fear that their leaders will sell out, will so enjoy the perquisites of leadership including the chance to associate with those of high social and political prestige that they will too readily compromise the demands of the workers. Coming from a particular economic class is not regarded as a guarantee that one will represent faithfully that class's interests. This anxiety about leaders' class loyalty is due not only to the experience of some trade union movements whose leaders have sold out, but also to the recognition that leaders, simply by virtue of being leaders, enter a different class. To be effective, they must give up their former occupation and work full time at their leadership tasks. They are no longer miners or farmers or plumbers. They begin to associate more with other leaders who come from other classes than they do with men of their former occupation. They may adopt the life style of a higher class and be more concerned to win this class's praise for being "responsible" leaders than to press the demands of their followers regardless of whether this causes leaders from other classes to condemn them. If leaders drawn from lower-class occupations are not seduced away from advocating their class's interest, the fact that they had the interest, drive, ability, or whatever to become leaders would still mean that they would differ from their followers in some significant way even though the two groups were matched exactly on a long list of attributes. Leaders can never represent their followers in the sense of mirroring them.

This is not to say that the working class never can trust its leaders just as higher-status classes cannot be certain that some of their members will not adopt a working-class cause as their own. Rather, the point is that the mere fact that leaders share a number of characteristics does not make them a monolithic group. They may conflict with each other. When they do, they are quite likely to seek further strength by attempting to enlist the support of those who are not part of the leadership group. To succeed, they will have to offer the nonleaders something in return for their backing. And if those whose support is sought do not find the proffered payoff sufficiently attractive, they can search for a more acceptable bargain from another group of leaders. Thus, not only will nonleaders have some of their interests attended to, but they will gain in some circumstances the power to govern—the power to choose between alternatives. Those who occupy leadership positions are a relatively small group with similar characteristics and attributes which are atypical of their society; this does not, however, make them a power elite. They may well not possess the power to decide what course of action will be authoritative policy for the system they lead.

And even if they have this power, the scope of their choice might well be limited by the desires and expectations of nonleaders. These desires and expectations, whether explicitly communicated to leaders or merely assumed by them to exist, may rule out certain courses of action and reduce leaders' maneuverability, thus to some extent structuring leaders' decisions. Their effect upon the political process turns not on whether the regents mirror or reflect the citizens' characteristics, but on whether desires and expectations are backed by effective sanctions. The key aspect of leadership responsibility is not representation but control. Those who make and implement authoritative policy, those who direct the processes of expressing and focusing demands for such policy are necessarily a relatively small, unrepresentative group. But this does not mean that they cannot be subject to the control of a sizable portion of the total citizenry.

Some students of politics regard this possibility as a forlorn hope. Even in a democracy, they contend, leaders are so able to control communication that they are virtually assured that most people will receive little derogatory information about them. Failures of policy may never come to light at all or, if they do, may be presented as qualified successes. In most cases the majority will be unaware that they are being had. Phrases like "management of the news" and "credibility gap" suggest the dimensions of the problem. This problem should not be minimized, but it must be understood that it is another of those charges, like the elite rule hypothesis, which is almost incapable of disproof and, to that extent, nonsense. Perhaps people really do have all the accurate information they need to make up their minds and really are satisfied with their political leaders. Or, while they may object to a few specific policies, they may be sufficiently pleased by a number of other decisions on matters they consider of crucial importance to feel that their leaders are acceptable. Or, despite being more dissatisfied than satisfied, they may not be so certain they are right and their leaders wrong —not because they lack information but because public problems are so complex that deciding what action is best is extremely difficult—that they are willing to oppose their leaders. The mere fact that a country does not have perpetual street riots does not mean that the politicians have duped the people. This is what makes the control-of-information argument a dubious one. Almost the only evidence which could disprove it would be for an electorate to defeat every politician every time he stood for re-election. Otherwise, the charge could be made that they allowed him to remain in office only because he had kept them from learning the truth about him.

The measure of effective control over political leaders is not the magnitude and severity of conflict between leaders and followers, but the treatment of those who oppose leaders. If most people are satisfied with leaders and their policies, few will dissent. Adequate control of leaders requires, however, that channels of communication be readily available for those who do wish to dissent and that those who avail themselves of these channels are not so persecuted that they and others are discouraged from opposing prevailing policies and leaders. The pertinent inquiry is whether evidence exists that dissent is permitted and protected as legitimate political behavior. Are journalists imprisoned for writing stories critical of the government's policies? Are legislators permitted only to praise the government? Are suggested alternative policies refuted on their merits or dismissed by impugning the motives of their proposers and stigmatizing them as cowards and virtually traitors?

Enforcement of leadership responsibility requires not only that dissenters be allowed to communicate their views to others; they must also be permitted to attempt to make their beliefs effective by forming structures that seek to influence or control the government. This freedom benefits not only those who wish to oppose existing policies and leaders; it serves the rest of the public as well. Democracy requires that leaders compete for office to give voters the opportunity to choose between alternative leaders and policies. In providing such contests periodically, parties make choice possible and thus help to control leaders. It has been contended, however, that parties must be democratic in order to serve as effective checks upon leaders. Members must be able to participate actively in determining party policy, and leaders must be responsive to their followers' preferences. This argument is the product of unthinking advocacy of democracy—for, if party leaders were responsible to their followers, they would short-circuit their responsibility to the voters.[8]

To illustrate this point, suppose that the Republican candidate for President in 1968 had campaigned for American withdrawal from Vietnam and that a majority of the voters, favoring this policy, had voted for him. After his inauguration, the Republican National Committee, having consulted extensively with state party organizations, resolved that the United States should escalate the war. The President, being a good democrat, was responsible to his party and followed a policy diametrically opposed to that on which he was elected. Intraparty democracy would have made a farce of electoral democracy.

Party members must recognize that their primary task is not to formulate party policy. Rather, they are to maintain the party machinery and operate it in accord with the leaders' plans so that the leaders will have an effective vehicle for presenting themselves and their policies to the voters for approval or rejection. Paradoxically, a democracy requires nondemocratic parties; ironically, this is true only where the party system is competitive. Where this is not the case, the dominant party must be democratic and must offer some competition between leaders and opportunities for dissent within the party structure, since the voters are presented little or no choice. In fact, it is only insofar as their dominant parties do provide this to some extent that some one-party regimes in developing countries can avoid being labeled oligarchies or dictatorships. But where leadership competition has been institutionalized between parties rather than within a dominant party, democratic party organization is less necessary and in fact is undesirable.

Merely to permit dissenters from prevailing policies to form new political structures that seek to influence or control the government may sound like a hollow opportunity, as is to tell someone who does not like either the Democrat or Republican candidate that he can form his own political party. Those who must form a party from scratch are at a tremendous disadvantage. Still, the obstacles are not insurmountable. Although the circumstances admittedly were exceptional (but then, circumstances always are), the Republican party won the United States' Presidency only six years after it was founded. And the Nazis, a less happy example, came to power in Germany only about twelve years after they were organized. Groups that embody the values and desires of a substantial number of people may well make rapid progress in obtaining political power.

The rapidly mounting expense of political campaigns, either in support of a candidate or in advocacy of a policy, does, however, make forming political groups much more difficult and tends to restrict political participation even, and more important especially, by those who are dissatisfied. To that extent the cost of politics threatens the effectiveness of popular control. Some countries have partially palliated this danger by using public revenues to pay some electoral expenses. Major political parties are given free radio and television time in Britain during election campaigns and at other times, and each candidate for Parliament is permitted to send one postage-free circular to every voter in his constituency. In France the government pays the costs of printing circulars and posters, up to a given level, and provides free poster sites.

These are examples of the steps which can be taken to help give citizens who are dissatisfied with the existing leaders and policy choices an opportunity to propose alternatives for public acceptance. However, these remedies are not only insufficient to solve the problem, but have defects of their own. Is it fair to require, as these countries do, that a candidate receive a certain percentage of the vote or that a party have a certain level of support before these aids are available? Does this not discriminate precisely against those who need financial support most? Alternatively, must the government provide financial support for the campaign of every crackpot who decides to run for office? And what about parties and candidates who advocate destroying the existing political system and replacing it with another—must they be aided as well? Comparative research can reveal what success various countries have had in dealing with such problems and can help to clarify the strengths and weaknesses of these measures. Research helps to provide a more rational basis for judging whether adoption of a particular measure would be likely to facilitate popular control of leaders without producing a number of negative side effects.

The fact that avoidance of elite rule requires everyone to have an opportunity to oppose leaders and their policies and to organize with others for this purpose does not mean that most people in a democracy will or should avail themselves of these opportunities.[9] Contrary to civics textbooks, a certain level of citizen political apathy may be desirable. If virtually everyone believed that politics was life's supreme pursuit, political conflict might well become highly explosive. Since people normally are least willing to compromise on matters they regard as most fundamental, to agree with a political opponent on a program of action might well seem to require betraying one's principles. In such circumstances people would be likely to cling dogmatically to their own proposals for government policy and suspect each other's motives. Society could be fractionalized into hostile, suspicious, noncommunicating sects unable to settle their differences peacefully within the existing political system. Moderate, balanced political interest and activity would seem to be more conducive to a healthy, stable democracy.

You may recall that I distinguished earlier between the self-confident citizen of the civic culture and the activist of the participant culture. The latter's zealous political commitment can be a divisive influence that threatens to disrupt his political system. The self-confident citizen, on the other hand, by combining the roles of the parochial, the subject, and the participant, possesses sufficient political interest, knowledge, and feelings of efficacy to participate in politics often and extensively enough to require leaders to pay attention to his interests without becoming so involved in politics that he strains the consensus and feelings of trust essential to a viable democratic system. The existence of opportunities to participate effectively when people wish to do so is more essential for democracy than frequent popular participation in politics. The possibility of such action serves as a sanction upon leaders' behavior and helps to make them popularly responsible.

In avoiding rule by the rich and the well-born, responsible government to some extent sacrifices rule by the able. To increase responsibility is to increase self-government; as self-government is maximized, so is the probability that mistakes will be made because the opportunities for men of average, rather than expert, knowledge and abilities to choose grow with self-government.

This sacrifice will seem a pity to most people and be regarded by some as too great a price to pay. Although most object vehemently to the idea of either of the first two categories monopolizing the power to make authoritative decisions, few want to entrust the government to incompetents. Thus the chimera of rule by the able has attracted people for centuries—the most perfect form of government of which Plato could conceive was rule by philosopher-kings. If a country were able to achieve a meritocracy, however, it would not be likely to be as satisfied or halcyon as many people would anticipate.[10] Errors in governing doubtless would be fewer, but self-government would be thwarted and essential opportunities for the growth of human maturity denied.

On my office wall hangs a photo of a wood carving by Arnold Flaten entitled "Paternalism." The top figure in this totem-like object wears a benign but somewhat condescending smile. One of his hands rests comfortingly on the head of the figure below him; the other hand grasps the lower figure's throat. Thus strangled, the lower figure's face is distorted horribly—eyes bulging and mouth contorted. Despite his beneficent intentions, indeed because of them, the upper figure is destroying the lower.

Every teenager knows the desire to be allowed to decide for himself more frequently, to be granted more important responsibilities more often. Only by deciding for himself, making errors and learning from them for the future, can he mature. So also with political life, people can mature only when they are responsible for governing themselves. They must have the chance to choose even though they will make mistakes.

For the anxious, the insecure, and those without guiding principles, the possibility of wrong choice is too great a risk. They cannot bear to be fully responsible for their choices, to be unable to shift the blame for their failure to someone else. For these people, self-government and freedom become intolerable burdens. They yearn for the security of the parental embrace despite its smothering confinement They may relinquish gladly the opportunity to govern themselves, preferring to follow the commands of a self-assured, more than human, leader, as Erich

Fromm in *Escape from Freedom* explains many Germans did in the 1930s. These insecure people believe that such a leader's insight and knowledge enables him to choose more wisely for them than they could for themselves; he spares them the anguish of decision and the risk of error. Thus, some people do not seek self-government; they flee from it. In so doing they cripple themselves, make themselves less than human. Here, once again, we see the importance of the self-confident citizen to responsible government. He is not fearful, but assured and ready to play his role in seeking to call leaders to account. A substantial number of such citizens must be moderately active in politics if elite rule is to be avoided.

In the last two generations the scope and degree of governmental power, especially that wielded by executive and administrative officials, have increased immensely. Those who exercise this power are exceptional individuals; they do not represent the population of their societies in the sense of mirroring modal characteristics or attributes. The fear that these individuals might, even in democratic countries, become an elite group controlling the political process to their own benefit has troubled people as different as President Eisenhower and John K. Galbraith, not to mention the most noted proponent of this thesis, C. Wright Mills. However, evidence is lacking that a tightly knit power elite governs even democratic political systems; the pluralistic view that those who make key political decisions vary from one issue and time to others seems more accurate. Nonetheless, those who decide authoritatively for a society remain a small, atypical segment of that society. Even in a pluralistic political system, government is by regents. Since it is unrealistic to expect that everyone can have a turn at being regent, the basic aim of a democratic political system must be to make the regents responsible to as broad a segment of the society as possible. Therefore, one of the fundamental inquiries of political science is: How is this to be done?

The answer does not lie in building a better constitution. The democratic phrases of the Soviet Union's constitution do nothing to control its political elite and Germany's Weimar constitution, hailed in its day as the most democratic ever written, collapsed in little more than a decade to the Nazi regime. Rather, what is needed are political structures and political cultures supportive of democracy. Cultures and structures may be influenced by institutions, but it is the former whose effect upon the political process is greatest. Decentralized government may help to prevent a dangerous concentration of power in the hands of a few political leaders; whether government is decentralized depends considerably more on role expectations than on legal arrangements. And, to cite another instance, the possibility of a military coup in the United States is infinitesimal not because it would be illegal, but because American military officers are products of a political culture that severely condemns such behavior. Thus these officers obey even when they believe the decisions of their civilian political superiors are wrong. Unlike officers in many developing countries, they do not conceive of their role as including periodic intervention into politics to clean up the mess produced by the politicians.

Among the structures helping to maintain democracy are parties capable of keeping political conflict within peaceful bounds and shaping political debate by formulating a limited number of policy alternatives acceptable to a broad segment of society. Because of their narrow, ideological appeals, parties in an extreme multiparty system are less able to fulfill this coalition-building function. Failure to reconcile diverse interests in such a system hinders the development of consensus and jeopardizes democracy. Parties also are more apt to succeed in aggregating interests if these are expressed through associational rather than nonassociational or institutional groups. Then assessment of the level of support for various alternatives is less difficult and opponents are less likely to be intransigent.

The cultures and structures supportive of democracy thrive in a society of self-confident citizens. These citizens are not zealous partisans or perpetual activists; such a high level of involvement could easily so intensify and embitter political conflict that it would destroy the consensus fundamental to democracy. Instead, the self-confident citizen is moderately interested in politics, trusts his fellow citizens to the extent of being able to work with them to secure political objectives, and feels that he would be able to influence the government if he attempted to do so.

While a highly developed economy creates conditions that help to produce structures and cultures favorable to democracy, it does not result automatically in a democratic political system. A modern social system not only has greater potential for democracy than does a traditional system; ironically, it also has a greater potential for totalitarian government. Furthermore, the process of economic modernization seems less conducive now to democratic development than it was in the past. In Western countries with a democratic tradition, industrialization began largely independently of the government The process thus generated new power centers which were able to check absolute government and whose rise to political power helped to create a precedent for subsequent expanding opportunities for political participation. Countries now seeking to modernize their economies wish to proceed more rapidly than did early industrializers. The costs of development are much greater and the ultimate goal a more complex economy than that attained by nineteenth-century industralization. Unlike their predecessors, contemporary developing nations are seeking to modernize their economies while simultaneously building their nation into an integrated system. Thus the government's role in developing these countries' economies is much greater than was true in those Western nations with a democratic tradition. The modernization process is much less likely, therefore, to spawn political structures and cultures productive of responsible government.

Developing countries will also find it difficult to avoid the danger of revolution. The hopes of their people for a better life are much more optimistic than were the expectations of the common people in the older nations at a comparable stage of development. Thus they are more likely to be disappointed and frustrated—a potentially revolutionary situation. Since most of the developing nations are new political systems whose legitimacy is not firmly established, their populations may very well express their frustrations by violently challenging the government's authority. Feelings of political competence would help to legitimate the political system, but this probably would require expanding significantly the opportunities for political participation. When, however, political structures are not durable, well-established, and adaptable yet autonomous, which typically is the case in developing nations, they can easily collapse under the pressure of greatly expanded participation.

The existence of such problems counsel against judging developing countries too harshly for failing to be democratic. In a new nation where national unity is not yet firmly established, a competitive party system might fragment the nation. A single party with a limited franchise might be a more hopeful strategy both for building a unified nation and for developing durable political structures. Yet the single-party system easily lends itself to oppression and manipulation of the people. Whether the one usage or the other predominates seems almost fortuitous, a matter of a leader's personality. Some nations have Ataturks and Nyereres, and others have Nkrumahs. The values these leaders instill in the people—intentionally or not—and the political structures which become established under their rule determine the future form of the political system, just as the values and structures prevalent in more developed countries affect their political processes and contribute either to democratic or to elite rule.

Chapter 7

Research Goals

for Comparative Politics

Throughout this book I have emphasized structures and functions, stressing that *structure* is a much broader term than *institution* or *organization*, since it includes the concepts of system and role. I have compared and contrasted the way in which and the extent to which structures in various types of political systems fulfill the functions of expressing, filtering, and focusing demands for authoritative decisions upon governmental structures, and I have examined the impact of structures whose primary purpose is to prescribe how a society shall employ its resources or to implement such prescriptions. Thus the approach I have used has been that of structural functional analysis.

This has been structural functionalism at only a moderately sophisticated level, however; I have not followed it to its chief concern—the matter of functional requisites.[1] In the first chapter I commented that all political systems have the same purpose —to decide authoritatively for a society—and that this book would be concerned primarily with examining the structures performing the functions basic to this central task. Although I described these functions, I did not explain in detail how they were basic. The distinctive feature of structural functionalism is to argue that certain functions are basic because a system cannot survive if they are not performed. True, structural functionalism is concerned with efficiency as well as with system maintenance (of course, these two concerns are interrelated since serious and persistent inefficiency is likely to jeopardize a system's viability); the second emphasis, however, is the one which integrates the approach. Whether inefficient performance of a function is significant turns upon whether that function is requisite to a system's continued existence.

By directing attention to the structures that fulfill a system's functional requisites, structural functionalism facilitates discovery of vestigial structures, which can be discarded, and malfunctions, which need to be rectified by modifying existing structures or establishing new ones. Thus this approach permits "job evaluations" of particular structures and rating of political systems according to their success in fulfilling their functional requisites. To this extent structural functional analysis would help to solve the predicament of whether normative statements are permissible in political science. Value judgments could be made on a more objective basis than mere personal preference.

This approach cannot solve the problem completely, for it should not be thought of simply as a political variety of time and motion study. Structural functionalism does not render obsolete the cardinal question in political science—Who governs? This approach is a means of clarifying the functions and structures involved in governing so that political scientists can ascertain more readily and accurately who in fact does govern and what means they employ in governing. The structural functionalist should inquire not only whether a society is maintaining itself efficiently, but also whether the structures it employs to fulfill its functional requisites favor self-government. Do these structures aid the maximum amount of popular participation consonant with maintenance of the system? Do they readily enable citizens to call the regents to account without hindering decisive making and implementation of authoritative decisions?

Such concerns obviously arise from particular value commitments.

The weakness of structural functionalism is the difficulty of determining what functions are requisite. If the basic argument of structural functionalism is correct, a single list of functional requisites should suffice for all political systems. Even if one were sufficiently lenient to permit different lists to be proposed for different types of systems, lists drawn up by different people for the same society should agree—a function cannot be requisite if it can be omitted from a list of tasks which must be performed for a society to continue to exist. The various lists that have been proposed, however, do not agree. While the differences between them are sometimes primarily semantic, they are frequently substantive. Thus the functional requisites themselves, despite their proposers' denials, come dangerously near to being personal preferences.

Part of the problem is the need to distinguish between functions which must be performed to maintain the entire society or social system and functions which are essential to the continued operation of the political system. If a society is to continue to exist, its members must be able to reproduce themselves. Since this is a requisite for society as a whole, there would be little point in repeating it as a requisite for a political system, although clearly the latter could not function without personnel. Perhaps in the case of politics one needs to reformulate this function in terms of the need for procedures to recruit new leaders into the political system. Furthermore, social and political requisites are also difficult to separate because the viability of the political system affects the social system. A social system that lacked a political system is virtually impossible to imagine; in that sense the political system is a requisite for the social system. And a political system which was constantly changing due to failure to perform its requisite functions would be highly likely to jeopardize the existence of the social system.

The comment about chronically unstable political systems suggests a final problem involved in devising lists of functional requisites. It may sound as though this concern is simply a new approach to the study of revolutions. This is not what structural functionalists intend. Their concern is broader than seeking the conditions which bring about violent overthrow of governments. Given the great difficulty which students of revolutions encounter in discovering the factors common to revolutions, the magnitude of the structural functionalists' task should be apparent. And if they are not to derive their list of functional requisites from examining particular political systems, they must rely on logic. This is better, of course, than personal preference, but not much more likely to secure agreement upon a single list of functions.

This is why I did not carry further my introductory remarks about the structural functional approach. I wished to use the approach as a general perspective or orientation to the study of comparative politics without becoming involved in the contentious question of whether functional requisites can be specified and, if so, what they are. This would have been an unnecessary detour. Now that I have demonstrated the usefulness of this approach, I will comment upon its potential utility in political inquiry beyond the scope of this book.

I have little hope that an agreed list of functional requisites will be attained in the near future. This problem will remain a serious flaw in the structural functional approach; it does not, however, vitiate it. All that can be done is for each political scientist using this approach to justify as thoroughly as possible the list of functions he intends to examine. Varying lists are an obstacle to comparability of research results, to say nothing of achieving the goal of structural functionalism, so, hopefully, political scientists will endeavor to use similar lists to maximize comparability.

Regardless of the extent to which this occurs, structural functionalism will remain valuable as a heuristic device. By generating new insights into the political process, suggesting questions for research, and offering new criteria for collecting data, structural functionalism helps to avoid the legalisms and superficial concerns of the institutional approach. Furthermore, although it does abstract from reality and thus falsifies to some extent, it corresponds to reality to a reasonable degree. These virtues must not obscure Oran Young's point that structural functionalism is not a theory, not "a statement of variables, relationships among variables, and predicted consequences of the interactions of the variables." [2] Structural functionalism does not offer an integrated set of empirically established or establishable hypotheses. The object of employing it in research is not to prove its validity, as would be the case with a theory, but rather to provide a way of selecting, organizing, and interpreting data—in brief to provide a perspective for study, to be a heuristic device. In a theory the key variables are empirically operationalized so that they can be investigated in explicit hypotheses. It is essential to do this in order to discover how change in one variable is related to another. Without variables there can be no hypotheses. Structural functionalism, which is an approach rather than a theory, has had great difficulty in operationalizing variables.

A good illustration of this is the work of Gabriel Almond. [3] Almond, one of the germinal figures in contemporary political science, has been grappling with this problem for well over a decade. He sketched his thinking on a structural functional approach to political research in "Comparative Political Systems" in 1956. Four years later, in the introduction to the book he edited with James Coleman, *The Politics of the Developing Areas*— a book which in many ways epitomizes the study of comparative politics in the 1960s—he elaborated his ideas into a conceptual framework. Then in 1965 in "A Developmental Approach to Political Systems," he revised this framework in the light of comments and criticisms. Subsequently, he utilized this revised scheme in *Comparative Politics: A Developmental Approach*, written with G. Bingham Powell, Jr.

The initial difficulty in applying Almond's approach could be attributed to the fact that it was a pioneering effort in political science and appeared in an edited volume. Almond had little control over the approach which each contributor to *The Politics of the Developing Areas* chose to employ to analyze the politics of those countries with which he was concerned. Thus it is not surprising that although they adopted some of his terminology, they did not utilize his approach as a framework for rigorous analysis. In the conclusion Coleman attempted, with limited success, to summarize the findings of the book's various area studies in terms of Almond's approach as a basis for generalization. This did not proceed much farther, however, than explaining what types of structures are characteristic of what types of political systems. The significance of such generalizations should not be minimized, although they do involve some danger of circularity. Insofar as one attempts to avoid defining transitional or developing societies in terms of geographical location or level of economic production, the distinguishing factor becomes the type of structures prevalent in a society. When the type of a society is defined this way, it is not surprising that all societies of that type have similar structures even though the structures referred to in the definition are social structures generally and those with which the political scientist is most concerned are political.

Little more could be done beyond what Coleman had accomplished because of the difficulty of operationalizing Almond's variables. For example, Almond argues that interests must be aggregated if a political system is to function successfully and that performance of this function is largely a matter for political parties. The problem is how to determine whether parties are sufficiently aggregative. The evidence is nothing so simple as the number of parties contesting elections. Both France and the Scandinavian countries have multiparty systems, yet parties in the latter seem to fulfill the aggregative function more satisfactorily. At any rate they do a better job of reconciling diverse interests, of building coalitions. This at least is what one would conclude from comparing these countries on government and cabinet stability and degree of trust across party lines. Perhaps these are the data to be used to determine whether parties are aggregative. Almond does not specify. Thus, while most people would agree that Scandinavian parties are more aggregative than French parties, and might also accept the view that Anglo-American parties are still more aggregative, such classifications remain rather imprecise matters of somewhat more or less and on balance because the variables have not been operationalized.

Or consider the variable of boundary maintenance. According to Almond, parties' primary function should be to aggregate interests and the various type of groups—associational, nonassociational, institutional, and anomic—should be involved chiefly in articulating interests. If the political system is to function efficiently each of these structures should stick to its own specialty —must remain within its functional boundaries—and prevent other structures from poaching on its functions. How structures are to perform this function and how one is to know whether they are doing so adequately is unclear. This is especially so when Almond has granted that all structures, even those in developed systems, are multifunctional to some extent. Almond provides no precise statement of how much multifunctionality in what structures is dysfunctional for a political system. Similarly, although various systems are distinguished in part according to substitutability of roles, this variable is not operationalized.

Almond's revisions of his approach have elevated it little closer to the level of a theory. Precise hypotheses of expected concomitant variations still have not been formulated, to say nothing of tested. The level of investigation remains that of static correlations between systems and structures. Even at this level the problem of operationalizing variables remains bothersome. One wonders whether several experts applying these concepts to the same group of countries would achieve the same results. Almond's examinations of various countries' political processes in these terms often seem to involve a considerable amount of personal judgment and to resemble plausible, after-the-fact explanations rather than verified hypotheses. Rather than arguing that the political processes of systems whose political structures differ in precise, operationalized characteristics should contrast in specified ways, Almond's approach seems to select political systems recognized to differ from each other and then to account for the differences in terms of his various functional concepts. The procedure is more ratiocinative than experimental. Perhaps this is in part because structural functionalism is more concerned to examine total systems than to study individual behavior. The number of total systems is so few, the number of cases in any one class likely to be so small, that explanations almost invariably will seem particularistic rather than statements of general relations.

I do not intend to imply that Almond is unaware of these difficulties, nor to minimize the value of his contribution. He is striving to make this approach more predictive and, therefore, verifiable. His writings have not only added to our understanding of comparative politics, but have also served to stimulate much other valuable research. His approach has considerable heuristic worth. But its virtues should not obscure its limitations. For it must be recognized that, in Gregor's words,

functional analyses are not explanatory at all—they are *analytic* and heuristic—and consequently singularly incapable, in themselves, of providing predictive or explanatory leverage. . . . They can pretend to explanatory power only when the initial suggestive analogy between society and . . . system is made sufficiently precise to render testable the formulation of empirical generalizations relating determinative variables in determinative relations.[4]

In the meantime, however, structural functionalism can serve to organize available knowledge, suggest research priorities, and strengthen research designs.

Perhaps it was in recognition of the limitations of structural functionalism that Almond in a recent study turned from concentrating on total systems to examining individual behavior patterns. In *The Civic Culture*, written with Sidney Verba and published in 1963, he investigated the political values, perceptions, and behavior of 5,000 persons from five countries to discover what type of political culture was most supportive of democracy and what factors were most capable of producing such a culture. Thus Almond was not abandoning his concern with total systems, but rather was attempting to explore systemic variety from another perspective.

Almond and Verba's chief inquiry in *The Civic Culture* was by no means new; the difference lay in their seeking to investigate the subject more rigorously than writers who had discussed it in the past, especially prior to the Second World War. Thus unlike James Bryce, for example, they were not content to rely on a chain of logic but sought empirical evidence to support expected logical connections. Does the political culture which logically is supportive of democracy in fact exist in stable democracies while absent from or tenuous in other systems? Do attitudes supportive of popular participation in politics prevail in countries where participation is high? Furthermore, do behavior and values correlate not just at the gross or macro level, but at the micro level as well? Is it not only true that American political culture favors participation and participation is relatively high, but also that those valuing participation most highly do in fact participate more than those valuing it less?

In answering such questions Almond and Verba included structural factors. Their chain of reasoning and evidence indicates that history—both individual personal history and national history—especially the level of technological development, shapes a society's structures, interpersonal attitudes, and political culture. The latter two factors are both related to the first, and all three influence political behavior. This in turn, along with structures and political culture, affects the type of the political system. The relations might be diagramed in the following manner:

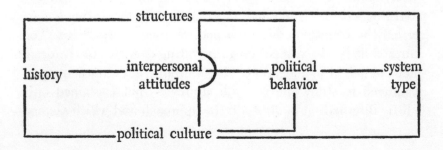

The fact that none of the connecting lines has arrow heads is a recognition of the reciprocal effects they have on each other. While interpersonal attitudes affect structure, for example, structures help to determine the quality of interpersonal attitudes.

Thus Almond and Verba sought, with partial success, to integrate behavioral with structural concerns. Almond's conceptual framework for structural functional analysis was not applied in *The Civic Culture*. Nonetheless, this study strongly emphasized the impact of interpersonal attitudes on structures and the effect of structures on the type of political system. When, for example, *The Civic Culture* discusses whether the level of interpersonal trust is sufficient to support the formation of associational groups and sustain broad political parties, it is clearly providing evidence on how successfully the articulation and aggregation functions are likely to be fulfilled. Thus the study of individual behavior can help to reveal the probable efficiency of political structures in fulfilling basic functions. Such study does not preclude, of course, the need to examine the structures to see whether they have taken full advantage of situations favorable to their functioning or have overcome obstacles to it. *The Civic Culture*, then, is only a beginning, for all the problems of vagueness of variables remain, but it is a significant start.

In evaluating the state of the study of comparative politics in the mid-1950s, Roy Macridis argued that the most pressing task was more adequate conceptualization.[5] He saw this as a means of correcting the many debilities which he correctly diagnosed. At the time this probably was good advice; certainly it was worth trying as an alternative or reform to what had been the dominant intellectual orientation of comparative government. Unfortunately political scientists have accepted this prescription too slavishly; a decade and a half devoted to conceptualizing has revealed the counterproductive aspect of such an emphasis. Too much time has been spent on formulating concepts to the detriment of actual investigation. The discipline has seen many prolegomena to study and research strategies that contained only a little information to illustrate the approach and which seemed rarely to be employed subsequently in actual investigation and analysis. Thus there developed the illusion that the discipline was advancing when in fact neither knowledge nor understanding was increasing.

Comparative politics needs to regain sight of the fact that a great deal can be accomplished without elaborate conceptualization or theorizing. This point can be illustrated well by contrasting the work of Hermens, or even Duverger, on electoral systems and party systems with that of Rae.[6] Hermens and Duverger advanced knowledge on this topic so little not because they failed to devise a brilliant conceptual framework, but because their methods were slipshod.[7] In contrast Rae investigates the subject thoroughly and rigorously. Although he develops some special measures and indices, he cannot be said to have elaborated a set of strikingly original or sophisticated concepts. The point is that he did not need to do so for his study to be valuable. Logic, rigor, testing of hypotheses instead of selective illustration, ambiguity, and lack of objectivity: these are the charcateristics distinguishing these works and making one a useful contribution and the others of limited worth.

Nor does Robert Alford's interesting study of class voting in Anglo-American political systems, *Party and Society*, involve any elaborate conceptualization.[8] The index of class voting, while original, is a rather simple measure of the behavior Alford wished to study. Yet by comparing thoroughly this aspect of politics in four political systems Alford was able to test some significant hypotheses and generate valuable insights into these systems' political processes. Had he spent his time in more adequate conceptualization, we would know less about class and politics than we do.

In addition to rigor and thoroughness in research, the other pressing need in comparative politics is for joint inquiry. No one man can be an expert on the politics of more than a handful of systems. The vogue for studying the developing nations, to correct the past European parochialism of comparative politics, has resulted in a rash of instant authorities—people who after a visit of only a few months to a country of which they previously know little presume to write detailed analyses of its political system. Merely increasing the number of comparative politics works about countries that are, to us, exotic, will not strengthen the discipline if these works are not written by people thoroughly conversant with these systems' structures and cultures. Clearly there must be joint effort.

And this joint effort must be of a different type from that which has prevailed. I have commented already on the failure of the contributors to Almond and Coleman's *The Politics of the Developing Areas* to employ rigorously Almond's conceptual framework in their area studies. Rather than being unique, this is almost universal behavior. Two more recent examples are *Political Oppositions in Western Democracies*, edited by Robert Dahl, and *Party Systems and Voter Alignments*, edited by Seymour Lipset and Stein Rokkan.[9] The subjects these volumes cover are extremely significant and deserve extensive investigation. While the essays' quality varies, most of them are thoroughly done and informative. The problem is that their findings are almost impossible to compare; each authority followed his own interests, with the result that the methods, the topics covered, the questions investigated vary greatly from one essay to another. The editors are left with the task of somehow demonstrating that all this diverse material really is interrelated. While their attempts to synthesize produce stimulating and sophisticated results, their essays do not draw closely upon the individual country studies.

Proceeding in this fashion can be a valid means of investigating a topic on which little is known. An agreed research framework might be too constricting. Allowing each expert to stress those facets of the topic which seem most important to him may yield considerably more information and provide the basis for a more valuable synthesis. But this way of proceeding presupposes that a second volume, at least, will follow in which the synthesis derived from the varied individual studies will be applied. In other words, once the initial ignorance on the topic has been dispelled somewhat so that we know what questions are worth asking and what hypotheses worth testing, a common research design needs to be applied to a group of countries to discover what is common and what unique and how these results are to be explained. Judging from past experience one can have little hope that this will occur. The syntheses which the editors of these volumes of collected essays labor over so diligently are not rigorously applied; the second volume never appears. Their efforts are not wasted, for they do stimulate thinking on the topic covered. Some other political scientists may even adopt one or two of their ideas for his research. And the editors themselves may try to use their product in their own research.

This falls far short, however, of the potential value of these efforts; it truly squanders our resources. Admittedly the differences between nations are so great and the amount of information available about them so varied that the same research design will not be applicable to all. Yet these disparities are often more an excuse than a reason. Surely when, as is the case in the Dahl volume, the nations included are all modern, developed Western democracies specifically selected because they were expected to have some political patterns in common, variations cannot be so great as to preclude further truly collective research from this foundation. Yet we are frequently told that we cannot expect mature scholars to give up their own approaches and merge their efforts in a single research framework. I fail to understand why political science research must be so individualistic. Collective inquiry is the predominant pattern in the physical sciences. This is not because everyone agrees about what approaches or ideas are most likely to be fruitful; joint research in the physical sciences is not a harmonious utopia. One need only read James Watson's *The Double Helix* to abandon that notion.[10] The physical sciences are able to combine diverse personalities with varying ideas into effective research units. Political science has not proceeded much beyond a few double harnessed teams (the Survey

Research Center group at the University of Michigan is an exception) and even these usually combine experts on the same country.

While a joint research team is the ideal, political science would be strengthened even if individual research were less idiosyncratic. A political scientist does not need to be a member of a research team to attempt to replicate in another country with which he is familiar someone else's earlier study. Now that data on voting behavior in Western Europe is becoming more widely available it should be possible for someone to test Alford's findings in these countries. Are they valid only for Anglo-American systems or do they apply to Western democracies more generally? Similarly, the many findings about legislative voting behavior in the American Congress and state legislatures could be used to guide research on other nations. Duncan Macrae, Jr., recently employed the techniques he developed in studying American legislatures in investigating parliamentary behavior during the French Fourth Republic.[11] This, however, is virtually an isolated example.[12] Why cannot someone specializing in Italian politics replicate Macrae's study in Italy during the same time period? Why should Macrae have to retool—learn enough about the Italian system to be able to do the job adequately? Another illustration of the unbelievable gaps in our basic knowledge due to failure to replicate is the fact that parliamentary voting in Canadian and Australian legislatures has never been studied thoroughly.[13] These are not obscure political systems where language, culture, and lack of records hamper research. Some of the hypotheses about legislative voting in Britain and the United States certainly could be tested in Canada and Australia, thereby strengthening our knowledge and understanding of all these political systems.

Speaking not of darkest Africa or Asia but of Western Europe, the Social Science Research Council's Committee on Research in Comparative Politics observed in the mid-1950s,

there are legal institutions and processes about which literally nothing is known. Second, for the most part our knowledge of formal governmental institutions is primarily historical and legal in character, and there have been relatively few studies of the actual functioning of these institutions. Third, there is the whole field of the nonlegal political institutions and processes—parties, pressure groups, public opinion —where research is only in its beginnings. And finally, these areas of ignorance, differences in approach, and unevennesses of development make difficult if not impossible those higher levels of comparative analysis without which genuine understanding is impossible . . . a scholar concerned with comparing even on a purely formal basis the organization of governmental powers for the continental European countries would find whole areas in which the basic data are lacking on the legal structure.[14]

In the rush to appear sophisticated by elaborating conceptual frameworks, this part of the committee's report was minimized. Obviously conditions have not remained static in the last decade and a half. Despite improvement, however, the committee's comments remain a fairly accurate description of the state of our knowledge. There is, then, a considerable amount of data collecting and analysis which urgently needs to be accomplished. Much of it requires no elaborate conceptualization.

I am not arguing that we can jettison concepts. Data collection must be informed if it is to attain its maximum utility; one cannot mindlessly gather information on everything and hope to obtain meaningful results. The significance of empirical discoveries can be heightened by relating them to structural concerns, as is clear from *The Civic Culture*. Political scientists do need a perspective on the political process so that they will know what priority to give to various possible research projects, what questions to ask, and where to look for evidence. Structural functionalism can provide all this, by directing attention to structures and their role in the political process, particularly if, granting its limitations, it is recognized as an approach rather than being forced to masquerade as a theory. Political scientists need to admit that their discipline is still largely in the natural history stage. We must still do a good deal of classifying in seeking to discover similarities and contrasts so that we can accumulate empirical generalizations. This task may not sound as exalted as constructing theory, but it is essential in order to reach that stage and, given present circumstances, it is a much more realistic objective.

Notes

CHAPTER 1

1. Albert Somit and Joseph Tanenhaus, "Trends in American Political Science," *American Political Science Review*, LVII (December 1963), 941–42.
2. This section draws upon the work of a number of authors. Leading examples of this approach are: Gabriel Almond and James Coleman, eds., *The Politics of Developing Areas* (Princeton University Press, 1960); David Easton, "An Approach to the Analysis of Political Systems," *World Politics*, IX (April 1957), 383–400; David Apter, "A Comparative Method for the Study of Politics," *American Journal of Sociology*, LXIV (November 1958), 221–37; and D. F. Aberle, *et al.*, "The Functional Prerequisites of a Society," *Ethics*, LX (January 1950), 100–11.

CHAPTER 2

1. Material for this discussion and the table are drawn from Lyle Shannon's "Is Level of Development Related to Capacity for Self-Government?" *American Journal of Economics and Sociology*, XVII (July 1958), 367–82. Shannon's study covered 88 independent political systems and 110 dependent ones, 85 systems which fell between the extremes of economic development by Shannon's measure are excluded from the first part of the table.
2. The leading studies on this topic are: Seymour Lipset, "Some Social Requisites of Democracy: Economic Development and Political Legitimacy," *American Political Science Review*, LIII (March 1959), 69–105; Gabriel Almond and James Coleman, eds., *The Politics of the Developing Areas* (Princeton University Press, 1960), pp. 538–44; Phillips Cutright, "National Political Development," *American Sociological Review*, XXVIII (April 1963), 253–64; Daniel Lerner, *The Passing of Traditional Society* (Free Press, 1958), pp. 54–64; Karl de

Schweinitz, Jr., *Industrialization and Democracy* (Free Press, 1964), pp. 23–34; and Deane Neubauer, "Some Conditions of Democracy," *American Political Science Review*, LXI (December 1967), 1002–09 and reply by Cutright and response by Neubauer in *American Political Science Review*, LXII (June 1968), 578–81. Cf. also Charles Wolf, Jr., *United States Policy and the Third World* (Little, Brown, 1967), pp. 96–103, 114–120.

3. *CPS* (M.I.T. Press, 1963) is an ambitious attempt to collect data on 57 characteristics, most of them political, for 115 independent countries. My measure of democracy combines characteristics 13, 26, 28, 29, 30, 41, 54, and 55. My economic condition index includes characteristics 7, 9, 11, and 12.

4. Spearman Rank Correlation Coefficient = .44, t with 104 d.f. = 4.97, significant at .001.

5. J. Lloyd Mechan, "Latin American Constitutions: Nominal and Real," *Journal of Politics*, XXI (May 1959), 258–75.

6. Ernest Hamburger discusses the provisions of these nations' constitutions in "Constitutional Thought and Aims in Former French Africa," *Social Research*, XXVIII (Winter 1961), 415–36.

7. Gabriel Almond and Sidney Verba, *The Civic Culture* (Little, Brown, 1965).

8. Hadley Cantril, *The Politics of Despair* (Collier Books, 1958).

9. Gabriel Almond, *The Appeals of Communism* (Princeton University Press, 1954), Chapter 10.

10. In addition to the previously cited Almond and Coleman and Almond and Verba studies, this discussion of political culture is based upon Almond's "Comparative Political Systems," *Journal of Politics*, XVIII (August 1956), 391–409; Lucian Pye, "The Non-Western Political Process," *Journal of Politics*, XX (August 1958), 468–86; and George Kahin, *et al.*, "Comparative Politics of Non-Western Countries," *American Political Science Review*, LXIX (December 1955), 1022–41.

11. I have not included a "traditional" category, within which countries like Saudi Arabia and Ethiopia would be classified, because so few political systems of this type still exist.

Labeling one of the main types of political systems "transitional" is not very satisfactory. It implies that all systems not of this type are stagnant and that all transitional systems are progressing inevitably from one stage of political development to another. I wish to imply neither, and use the term only because it is common in writings on this subject and no preferable term has been suggested yet. Thus my usage implies merely that transitional systems are losing many of the characteristics which formerly made them traditional systems and that they have begun this process more recently and, therefore, have carried it less far than those systems termed modern.

12. Lipset notes in his previously cited "Some Social Requisites of De-

mocracy," pp. 84–85, evidence from a number of other studies supporting this conclusion.

13. *Ibid.*, pp. 96–97 and studies there noted. Verba mentions other studies in "Organizational Membership and Democratic Consensus," *Journal of Politics*, XXVII (August 1965), 467–97, the article on which these two paragraphs are based.

The belief that people subject to cross-pressure tend to withdraw from politics by refusing to vote is challenged seriously by Pool, Abelson, and Popkin in *Candidates, Issues, and Strategies: A Computer Simulation of the 1960 and 1964 Presidential Elections* (M.I.T. Press, 1964), pp. 72–78. Their evidence suggests that this behavior occurs only when voters are repelled by the alternatives rather than attracted to them.

14. Seymour Lipset, *Political Man* (Doubleday, 1960), esp. pp. 50–113. James S. Coleman questions this generalization in *Education and Political Development* (Princeton University Press, 1965), pp. 19–20.

CHAPTER 3

1. This section is based primarily upon the following studies of political and economic development: Robert Holt and John Turner, *The Political Basis of Economic Development* (Van Nostrand, 1966), Barrington Moore, Jr., *Social Origins of Dictatorship and Democracy* (Beacon Press, 1966), A. F. K. Organski, *The Stages of Political Development* (Knopf, 1965), and Karl de Schweinitz, Jr., *Industrialization and Democracy* (Free Press, 1964). See also Friedrich Heer, *The Medieval World* (New American Library, 1963), Chapters 2 and 4.

2. On the dangers of rapid economic development for a democratic political system, see Samuel Huntington, "Political Development and Political Decay," *World Politics*, XVII (April 1965), 386–430; William Kornhauser, *The Politics of Mass Society* (Free Press, 1959); Seymour Lipset, *Political Man* (Doubleday, 1960).

3. In a study of Latin American countries Charles Wolf, Jr., found that while Gross National Product, Gross National Product per capita, gross investment, gross investment per capita, and per capita Gross National Product growth rate all had significant rank order correlations with level of democracy, Gross National Product growth rate and gross investment as a percentage of Gross National Product did not. He suggests that this finding can be interpreted as evidence that developing nations with democratic political systems have a more limited growth potential than those with dictatorial systems because in the former the wishes of the public must be followed more closely. Thus a greater proportion of national wealth must be allocated for present consumption rather than for capital concentration essential to investment for economic development. *United States Policy and the Third World* (Little, Brown, 1967), pp. 96–103 and 114–120. Joseph LaPalombara and Myron

Weiner argue, however, in *Political Parties and Political Development* (Princeton University Press, 1966), pp. 388–98 and 432–33, that the recent experience of developing countries has failed to demonstrate conclusively that an authoritarian political system produces more rapid economic development than do more liberal regimes.

4. In "Political Development and Political Decay," *loc. cit.*, Huntington argues that political systems decay rather than develop when participation increases so rapidly that institutionalization cannot keep pace. While his argument is persuasive and supported by several illustrations, it has not been substantiated yet by rigorous empirical research. The following three paragraphs in the text are based on Huntington's views.

5. "Comparative Political Systems," *Journal of Politics*, XVIII (August 1956), 408.

6. Merle Kling, "Towards a Theory of Power and Political Instability in Latin America," *Western Political Quarterly*, IX (March 1956), 21–35.

7. This discussion is based on the following sources: Hannah Arendt, *On Revolution* (Viking, 1963); Crane Brinton, *The Anatomy of Revolution* (rev. ed., Vintage, 1956); James Davies, "Toward a Theory of Revolution," *American Sociological Review*, XXVII (February 1962), 5–19; Andrew Janos, *The Seizure of Power*, research monograph No. 16 (Princeton: Center of International Studies, 1964); Chalmers Johnson, *Revolution and the Social System* (Hoover Institution, 1964); and Charles Tilly and James Rule, *Measuring Social Upheaval*, research monograph No. 19 (Princeton: Center of International Studies, 1965).

8. Significant as they are in helping to produce a revolutionary situation, economic frustrations are not the only dissatisfactions that can jeopardize government stability. Failure of a government to fulfill expected or desired hopes of national glory may stimulate revolutionary opposition. For example, France came close to revolution in 1958 in part because of the frustration of military defeat in Indo-China followed by the possibility of a negotiated settlement with the Algerian rebels. Thus my comments on the factors productive of revolution should not be interpreted as an argument for economic determinism.

9. Seymour Lipset, "Some Social Requisites of Democracy," *American Political Science Review*, LIII (March 1959), 86–88.

10. Some twentieth-century dictatorships also retained monarchical institutions in an effort to strengthen their legitimacy and attempted to solve the problem of the transfer of power in a dictatorship by involving the monarch in the process of leadership succession. Such a strategy is a dangerous one, however, for insofar as a monarch does command considerable loyalty, he may help to force a dictator out of power. Apparently, democratic structures can be manipulated more safely. Cf. John Herz, "The Problem of Successorship in Dictatorial Regimes; a Study in Comparative Law and Institutions," *Journal of Politics*, XIV (February 1952), 19–40.

11. Gabriel Almond and Sidney Verba, *The Civic Culture* (Little, Brown, 1965), Chapter 8.

CHAPTER 4

1. Gabriel Almond and Sidney Verba, *The Civic Culture* (Little, Brown, 1965), Chapter 2.
2. This discussion of those who participate in politics is based upon Almond and Verba; Seymour Lipset, *Political Man* (Doubleday, 1960); William Kornhauser, *The Politics of Mass Society* (Free Press, 1959); and Lester Milbrath, *Political Participation* (Rand McNally, 1965). Milbrath's work is by far the most thorough and comprehensive. Unfortunately, however, he does not always distinguish between findings based solely on American studies and those which have been validated in other countries also. Nor does he adequately differentiate cross-national and truly replicative studies from similar, but not strict comparative, research conducted in several countries.
3. Angus Campbell and Henry Valen, "Party Identification in Norway and the United States," *Public Opinion Quarterly*, XXV (Winter 1961), 505–25, and Stein Rokkan and Angus Campbell, "Norway and the United States of America," *International Social Science Journal*, XII: 1 (1960), 69–99.
4. Philip Converse and George Dupeux, "Politicization of the Electorate in France and the United States," *Public Opinion Quarterly*, XXVI (Spring 1962), 1–24.
5. Ecological correlations state the extent to which factors are associated on a gross basis within a given area, be it a constituency, a county, a precinct. Thus, for example, a study might try to relate the percentage of working-class people within each ward with the percentage of voters in that ward favoring the conservative candidate. The problem with this technique is that it attempts to generalize about individual behavior on the basis of data about the total group as a group rather than on the basis of data concerning each individual. The fact that it is a gross approach means that it really can reveal nothing with certainty about individual behavior, which in fact may be quite different and support contrary conclusions.
6. Robert Alford, *Party and Society* (Rand McNally, 1963). See also W. G. Runciman, "A Method for Cross-National Comparison of Political Consensus," *British Journal of Sociology*, XIII (June 1962), 151–55.
7. Seymour Lipset, "The Changing Class Structure and Contemporary European Politics," *Daedalus*, XCIII (Winter 1964), 271–303.
8. Austin Ranney and Willmoore Kendall elaborate this point in their *Democracy and the American Party System* (Harcourt, Brace, 1956), pp. 511–13.
9. The principal sources upon which I drew for information on electoral

systems were: Maurice Duverger, *Political Parties*, tr. by Barbara and Robert North (Wiley, 1954); Enid Lakeman and James Lambert, *Voting in Democracies* (Faber, 1955); John Grumm, "Theories of Electoral Systems," *Midwest Journal of Political Science*, II (November 1958), 357–76; and Giovanni Sartori, Chapter Five in Joseph La Palombara and Myron Weiner, eds., *Political Parties and Political Development* (Princeton University Press, 1966). See also Leslie Lipson, "Party Systems in the United Kingdom and the Older Commonwealth: Causes, Resemblances, and Variations," *Political Studies*, VII (February 1959), 12–31.

10. For a discussion of the logical failures and contradictions in Duverger's work, see Aaron Wildavsky, "A Methodological Critique of Duverger's *Political Parties*," *Journal of Politics*, XXI (May 1959), 303–18. In "Models, Theories, and the Theory of Political Parties," *Political Studies*, VII (June 1959), 127–46, Colin Leys attempts logically to salvage something of Duverger's theories of the relation between party systems and electoral systems.

11. James S. Coleman and Carl Rosberg, *Political Parties and National Integration in Tropical Africa* (University of California Press, 1964), concluding chapter, and Martin Kilson, "Authoritarian and Single Party Tendencies in African Politics," *World Politics*, XV (January 1963), 262–94.

12. The data cited here on former French and British colonies are from Arthur Banks and Robert Textor, *A Cross-Polity Survey* (M.I.T. Press, 1963), 80/139, 80/139M, and 80/113.

13. C. W. Cassinelli, "The Totalitarian Party," *Journal of Politics*, XXIV (February 1962), 111–41, and Aryeh Unger, "Party and State in Soviet Russia and Nazi Germany," *Political Quarterly*, XXXVI (October-December 1965), 441–59.

14. Charles Anderson, "Central American Political Parties: A Functional Approach," *Western Political Quarterly*, XV (March 1962), 125–39.

15. Joseph LaPalombara and Myron Weiner, eds., *Political Parties and Political Development* (Princeton University Press, 1966), concluding chapter.

16. Harry Eckstein, *Pressure Group Politics* (Stanford University Press, 1960); Henry Ehrmann, *Organized Business in France* (Princeton University Press, 1957); J. D. Stewart, *British Pressure Groups* (Clarendon Press, 1958); and Joseph LaPalombara, *Interest Groups in Italian Politics* (Princeton University Press, 1964).

17. For example, Henry Ehrmann, ed., *Interest Groups on Four Continents* (University of Pittsburgh Press, 1958).

18. Almond and Verba, *op. cit.*, pp. 148, 160.

19. Gabriel Almond and James Coleman, eds., *The Politics of the Developing Areas* (Princeton University Press, 1960).

20. Bruce Millin argues in *The Political Role of Labour in Developing Countries* (Brookings, 1962) that trade unions have considerable po-

litical influence in developing countries because, despite their weaknesses, they are one of the few organized groups that support the
government against the traditional leaders and they are a valuable
means of propagandizing. Elliot Berg and Jeffrey Butler in "Trade
Unions" in James Coleman and Carl Rosberg, Jr., eds., *Political
Parties and National Integration in Tropical Africa* (University of
California Press, 1964) maintain that in tropical Africa unions were
little involved in politics and had little impact when they were politically active before independence and have had little influence since
independence. Perhaps Millin is comparing implicitly unions' influence
with that of other associational groups, in which case it probably would
appear great. Certainly nothing in the studies in Almond and Coleman
suggests that unions are unimportant only in tropical Africa. Furthermore, since, as Millin admits, unions function as government agents
after the colonial ruler has granted independence, it is hard to see how
unions can exercise considerable autonomous influence.

21. Morris Janowitz, *The Military in the Political Development of New
Nations* (University of Chicago Press, 1964); S. E. Finer, *The Man on
Horseback* (Praeger, 1962); John Johnson, *The Military and Society in
Latin America* (Stanford University Press, 1964); John Johnson, ed.,
The Role of the Military in Underdeveloped Countries (Princeton
University Press, 1962); and Fred von der Mehden and Charles An-
derson, "Political Action by the Military in Developing Areas," *Social
Research*, XXVIII (Winter 1961), 459–79.

CHAPTER 5

1. See for example, Herbert J. Spiro's *Government by Constitution*
(Random House, 1959), which offers a set of "guidelines for constitu-
tion-makers."

2. For another argument that what matters in Britain is the party system,
not the institutions, see Martin Needler, "On the Dangers of Copying
from the British," *Political Science Quarterly*, LXXVII (September
1962), 379–96.

3. To note just a few such sources, Michel Ameller in *Parliaments* (rev.
ed.; Cassell, 1966) provides a detailed account of the organization and
procedures of the parliaments of 55 countries. Somewhat less systematic is K. C. Wheare's *Legislatures* (Oxford, 1963). Two books
which compile similar information on administration are A. L. Adu,
The Civil Service in New African States (Praeger, 1965) and Brian
Chapman, *The Profession of Government* (Allen & Unwin, 1959),
although the latter does go beyond description to discuss as well the
role of various European civil services. On judicial review in a few
foreign countries, see Taylor Cole, "Three Constitutional Courts: A
Comparison," *American Political Science Review*, LIII (December
1959), 963–84. For judicial systems more generally, Henry Abraham's

Courts and Judges (Oxford, 1959), and, for the United States, Britain, and France, his *Judicial Process* (Oxford, 1962). Sources on federalism additional to those mentioned in note 11 below are: A. H. Birch, *Federalism, Finance and Social Legislation in Canada, Australia and the United States* (Oxford, 1955); William Livingston, *Federalism and Constitutional Change* (Oxford, 1956); and Edward McWhinney, *Comparative Federalism* (University of Toronto, 1962).

4. Charles O. Jones, "Inter-party Competition in Britain—1950–1959," *Parliamentary Affairs*, XVII (Winter 1963–64), 50–56, and Jorgen Rasmussen, "The Implication of Safe Seats for British Democracy," *Western Political Quarterly*, XIX (September 1966), 516–29. For the United States, Charles O. Jones, "Inter-party Competition for Congressional Seats," *Western Political Quarterly*, XVII (September 1964), 461–76.

5. Leon Epstein, "British M.P.s and Their Local Parties: The Suez Cases," *American Political Science Review*, LIV (June 1960), 374–90, and Jorgen Rasmussen, *The Relations of the Profumo Rebels with Their Local Parties* (University of Arizona Press, 1966), Institute of Government Research Monograph, Comparative Government Studies, Number 1. See also Graeme Moodie, *The Government of Great Britain* (2nd ed.; Crowell, 1964), pp. 97–98.

6. In addition to the Epstein and Rasmussen studies cited in Note 5, Austin Ranney, *Pathways to Parliament* (University of Wisconsin Press, 1965).

7. Leon Epstein, "A Comparative Study of Canadian Parties," *American Political Science Review*, LVIII (March 1964), 46–59.

8. Nathan Leites, *On the Game of Politics in France* (Stanford University Press, 1959).

9. Allan Kornberg, "Caucus and Cohesion in Canadian Parliamentary Parties," *American Political Science Review*, LX (March 1966), 83–92, and "The Rules of the Game in the Canadian House of Commons," *Journal of Politics*, XXVI (May 1964), 358–80.

10. Robert McKenzie, *British Political Parties* (2nd ed.; Mercury Books, 1964).

11. William Riker, *Federalism* (Little, Brown, 1964). K. C. Wheare, *Federal Government* (4th ed.; Oxford University Press, 1963).

12. Jorgen Rasmussen, "A Research Note on Canadian Party Systems," *Canadian Journal of Economics and Political Science*, XXXIII (February 1967), 98–106.

13. Aaron Wildavsky, "Party Discipline under Federalism," *Social Research*, XXVIII (Winter 1961), 437–58.

14. My comments on bureaucratic structures are based primarily on about the only comprehensive assessment of comparative administration, Ferrel Heady's *Public Administration: A Comparative Perspective* (Prentice-Hall, 1966), with some further reference to John Armstrong,

"Sources of Administrative Behavior: Some Soviet and West European Comparisons," *American Political Science Review*, LIX (September 1965), 643–55; Ralph Braibanti, *et al.*, *Asian Bureaucratic Systems' Emergent from the British Imperial Tradition* (Duke University Press, 1966); and Richard Harris and Robert Kearney, "A Comparative Analysis of the Administrative Systems of Canada and Ceylon," *Administrative Science Quarterly*, VIII (December 1963), 339–60.

CHAPTER 6

1. Allan Kornberg and Norman Thomas, "The Political Socialization of National Legislative Elites in the United States and Canada," *Journal of Politics*, XXVII (November 1965), 761–75.
2. The following paragraphs are based upon Lester W. Milbrath's *Political Participation* (Rand McNally, 1965).
3. Sources relied upon for the following comments include: Gabriel Almond and James Coleman, eds., *The Politics of the Developing Areas* (Princeton University Press, 1960); James Coleman, ed., *Education and Political Development* (Princeton University Press, 1965); Yasumasa Kuroda, "A Cross-Cultural Analysis of the Desire for Political Power: Empirical Findings and Theoretical Implications," *Western Political Quarterly*, XX (March 1967), 51–64; Daniel Lerner, "The Coercive Ideologists in Perspective," in Harold Lasswell and Daniel Lerner, eds., *World Revolutionary Elites* (M.I.T. Press, 1965); Daniel Lerner, "Elite Research Procedures," in Harold Lasswell, *et al.*, *The Comparative Study of Elites* (Stanford University Press, 1952); Dankwart Rustow, "The Study of Elites," *World Politics*, XVIII (July 1966), 690–717; and Fred von der Mehden, *Politics of the Developing Nations* (Prentice-Hall, 1964).
4. The two best-known national studies of the United States are C. Wright Mills' *The Power Elite* (Oxford, 1956) and Floyd Hunter's *Top Leadership, U.S.A.* (University of North Carolina Press, 1959). A recent well-done study of power structure in another country is John Porter's *The Vertical Mosaic: An Analysis of Social Class and Power in Canada* (University of Toronto Press, 1965). Many of the American community power studies are cited in Nelson Polsby, *Community Power and Political Theory* (Yale University Press, 1963).
5. Delbert Miller, "Industry and Community Power Structure," *American Sociological Review*, XXIII (February 1958), 9–15, and William Form, "Integration and Cleavage Among Community Influentials in Two Border Cities," *American Sociological Review*, XXIV (December 1959), 804–14.
6. For a more thorough discussion of these points see Polsby, note 4, *supra*. An example of the decision-making approach to community power structure is Robert Dahl's *Who Governs?* (Yale University Press,

204 / The Process of Politics

1961). Dahl points out some of the logical deficiencies in the ruling elite hypothesis in "A Critique of the Ruling Elite Model," American Political Science Review, LII (June 1958), 463–69.

7. Maurice Duverger, *Political Parties* (Wiley, 1954), pp. 422–27.
8. This is the basic theme of Robert McKenzie's *British Political Parties* (2nd ed., Mercury Books, 1964).
9. This argument draws upon points made by Gabriel Almond and Sidney Verba in *The Civic Culture* (Little, Brown, 1965), and Milbraith, pp. 142–54, note 2, *supra*.
10. Michael Young's novel, *The Rise of the Meritocracy 1870–2033* (Penguin Books, 1961) explores some of the problems of rule by the able.

CHAPTER 7

1. Although Marion Levy, Jr., Talcott Parsons, and Robert Merton are the principal fountainheads for structural functionalism in political science, one who knows little about this approach would be better advised to consult the following references before turning to their works. D. F. Aberle, *et al.*, "The Functional Prerequisites of a Society," *Ethics*, LX (January 1950), 100–11; F. X. Sutton, "Social Theory and Comparative Politics," *Comparative Politics*, ed. by Harry Eckstein and David Apter (Free Press, 1963), pp. 67–81; Harry Eckstein, "A Perspective on Comparative Politics, Past and Present," *Comparative Politics*, pp. 26–29; David Apter, "Comparative Politics and Political Thought: Past Influences and Future Development," *Comparative Politics*, pp. 725–38; Oran Young, *Systems of Political Science* (Prentice-Hall, 1968); William Flanagan and Edwin Fogelman, "Functional Analysis," *Contemporary Political Analysis*, ed. James Charlesworth (Free Press, 1967), pp. 72–85; Robert Holt, "A Proposed Structural-functional Framework," *Contemporary Political Analysis*, pp. 86–107; and A. James Gregor, "Political Science and the Uses of Functional Analysis," *American Political Science Review*, LXII (June 1968), 425–39. Portions of H. V. Wiseman, *Political Systems* (Praeger, 1967) may be helpful also.
2. Young, *op. cit.*, p. 97. Young discusses some of this paragraph's points, pp. 8–12 and 95–99.
3. References for works mentioned in this paragraph are "Comparative Political Systems," *Journal of Politics*, XVIII (August 1956), 391–409; *The Politics of the Developing Areas* (Princeton University Press, 1960); "A Developmental Approach to Political Systems," *World Politics*, XVII (January 1965), 183–214; and *Comparative Politics: A Developmental Approach* (Little, Brown, 1966).
4. Gregor, *op. cit.*, p. 431.
5. Roy Macridis, *The Study of Comparative Government* (Random House, 1955).

6. Ferdinand Hermens, *Democracy or Anarchy?* (University of Notre Dame, 1941); Maurice Duverger, *Political Parties*, trans. Barbara and Robert North (Wiley, 1954); Douglas Rae, *The Political Consequences of Electoral Laws* (Yale University Press, 1967).

7. For a critique of Duverger's methods, see Aaron Wildavsky, "A Methodological Critique of Duverger's *Political Parties,*" *Journal of Politics*, XXI (May 1959), 303–18.

8. Robert Alford, *Party and Society* (Rand McNally, 1963).

9. Robert Dahl, ed., *Political Oppositions in Western Democracies* (Yale University Press, 1966) and Seymour Lipset and Stein Rokkan, eds., *Party Systems and Voter Alignments* (Free Press, 1967).

10. James Watson, *The Double Helix* (Atheneum, 1968).

11. Duncan Macrae, Jr., *Parliament, Parties, and Society in France 1946–1958* (St. Martin's Press, 1967).

12. Donald Stokes, in conjunction with David Butler, is endeavoring to utilize some of the methods which the Survey Research Center has employed so successfully in the study of voting behavior in the United States to investigate voting in Britain. The results of this effort have not yet appeared.

13. The only study for Canada which Leon Epstein could find ("A Comparative Study of Canadian Parties," *American Political Science Review*, LVIII [March 1964], 52, n. 25) was one contained in John Williams' *The Conservative Party of Canada 1920–1949* (Duke University Press, 1956), pp. 200–204, which focused on only one division for each of 28 years. While several books on Australian politics discuss party discipline, I have been unable to discover any study that examines party cohesion thoroughly.

14. Gabriel Almond, Taylor Cole, and Roy Macridis, "A Suggested Research Strategy in Western European Government and Politics," *American Political Science Review*, XLIX (December 1954), 1042–49.

For Further Reading

STUDENTS wishing to learn more about the topics discussed in this book could begin by reading the works cited in the footnotes. These works vary in importance and quality, however, so I will suggest additional readings most likely to be worthwhile. Doing so also will permit me to comment briefly on some works' significance and contents and will facilitate reference to some items not mentioned in the footnotes.

CHAPTER 1

The history of political science in the United States as sketched by Albert Somit and Joseph Tanenhaus in *The Development of American Political Science: From Burgess to Behavioralism* (Allyn & Bacon, 1967) while informative is probably of greatest value to those having some previous background in political science. More helpful to the newer student is Harry Eckstein's concise summary of the historical development of comparative politics in terms of its main intellectual movements in "A Perspective on Comparative Politics, Past and Present," the introduction to the reader, *Comparative Politics* (Free Press, 1963), edited by Eckstein and David Apter. Apter's concluding chapter for the same volume, "Comparative Politics and Political Thought: Past Influences and Future Development," focuses on postwar trends, especially behavioral and structural studies, and effectively supplements Eckstein's comments.

A good way to obtain perspective on current trends in comparative politics is to read Roy Macridis' assessment of the state of the field as of fifteen years ago—*The Study of Comparative Government* (Random House, 1955). Macridis also proposed a simple scheme of analysis to guide political research. He briefly evaluates more recent developments in comparative politics in "Comparative Politics and the Study of Government," *Comparative Politics*, I (October 1968). This issue also contains several other articles by prominent political scientists prescribing various approaches to the study of comparative politics and research goals.

Perhaps the best way to understand the scope and aims of political science is to read some of the many works that discuss a wide variety of approaches to the study of politics, conceptual frameworks, and methods and techniques of investigation. Among the more useful collections of essays on these subjects are James Charlesworth, ed., *Contemporary Political Analysis* (Free Press, 1967); Stephen Bailey, ed., *Research Frontiers in Politics and Government* (Brookings, 1955); Roland Young, ed., *Approaches to the Study of Politics* (Northwestern University Press, 1959); Austin Ranney, ed., *Essays on the Behavioral Study of Politics* (University of Illinois Press, 1962); Robert Farrell, ed., *Approaches to Comparative and International Politics* (Northwestern University Press, 1966); and Robert Connery, ed., *Teaching Political Science* (Duke University Press, 1965).

An appreciation of the diversity, accomplishments, and goals of political science also can be obtained by perusing many of the selections in some of the better readers. In addition to the Eckstein and Apter volume, two good collections of studies on comparative politics and foreign political systems are Roy Macridis and Bernard Brown, eds., *Comparative Politics* (3rd ed., Dorsey Press, 1968) and Henry Albinski and Lawrence Pettit, eds., *European Political Processes* (Allyn & Bacon, 1968).

CHAPTER 2

On the question of whether a certain level of economic development is a democratic requisite, the most significant studies are those cited in note 2 to this chapter, especially those by Lipset, Coleman, Cutright, and Neubauer. Although this chapter mentioned Lipset primarily regarding his research on this relation, he has not confined his studies on democratic stability to this point alone. His views on the significance of values for political legitimacy and democratic maintenance perhaps can be best understood by seeing how he relates them to the development of the American political system in *The First New Nation* (Basic Books, 1963).

In the latter part of this work he turns to comparative analysis to show how his views help to explain the status of democracy in several foreign political systems. In an introductory chapter to *Party Systems and Voter Alignments* (Free Press, 1967), he and Stein Rokkan attempt to demonstrate how different types and sequences of basic societal cleavages affect political stability. Stimulating as their discussion is, it is highly questionable whether it is relevant to non-West European political systems.

Almond and Verba's *The Civic Culture* (Little, Brown, 1965) is basic reading on the significance of value systems for democratic government. Contrasting to some extent with their effort to specify the values most conducive to democracy is Harry Eckstein's argument that the key issue is the extent to which political authority patterns are congruent with social authority patterns. He develops this idea for a specific political system—Norway—in *Division and Cohesion in Democracy* (Princeton University Press, 1966); an appendix to this book reprints his earlier "A Theory of Stable Democracy" in which he explained his views more abstractly with only illustrative references to various countries. Also stressing the importance of popular conceptions of political authority for democratic stability is Eric Nordlinger's *The Working-Class Tories* (University of California Press, 1967) which, despite its title, is concerned primarily with democratic requisites and discusses the French political system as well as the British.

Values and conditions essential to democracy also can be established by examining the nature of antidemocratic pathologies. In addition to Cantril's and Almond's works cited in notes 8 and 9 to Chapter 2, Ernst Nolte's *Three Faces of Fascism* (Holt, Rinehart & Winston, 1966) provides a good comparative perspective on antidemocratic movements of the right—although it differs from the other two works, being more a history of the movements' development than a discussion of interview data. Another informative—although at times simplistic—attempt to derive democratic essentials from the history of the collapse of democracies is Norman Stamps, *Why Democracies Fail* (University of Notre Dame Press, 1957). Many books discuss individual countries' intellectual heritage and value systems and relate this to democratic stability. Two that are especially noteworthy are Peter Viereck's *Metapolitics: The Roots of the Nazi Mind* (Capricorn Books, 1961); and Stanley Hoffman, ed., *In Search of France* (Harper & Row, 1965), especially the chapters written by Hoffman himself and Jesse Pitts.

The two chief inventories of economic, social, and political data available for attempting to relate types of political systems to specific sets of conditions are Arthur Banks and Robert Textor's *A Cross-Polity Survey* (M.I.T. Press, 1963) and Bruce Russett, *et al.*, *World Handbook of Political and Social Indicators* (Yale University Press, 1964). CPS tends to include more characteristics requiring subjective classifications but, as a result, also covers more clearly political characteristics. Some idea of the problems and potentialities of research employing such inventories can be gained from Richard Merritt and Stein Rokkan, eds., *Comparing Nations: The Use of Quantitative Data in Cross-National Research* (Yale University Press, 1966); and Phillip Gregg and Arthur Banks, "Dimensions of Political Systems: Factor Analysis of *A Cross-Polity Survey*," *American Political Science Review*, LIX (September 1965), 602–14. Another interesting attempt to relate social and economic data to political systems is Karl Deutsch, "Social Mobilization and Political Development," *American Political Science Review*, LV (September 1961), 493–514.

CHAPTER 3

The literature on political development is voluminous and varied. Surprisingly, however, most of it deals with non-Western countries; only recently have political scientists begun to recognize the need to study the process through which current Western systems evolved and to examine the extent to which the historical experience of these systems is relevant to contemporary non-Western systems. The two leading efforts are the Holt and Turner and the Moore works mentioned in note 1 to Chapter 3. Interestingly these two studies have opposite focal points of research. Moore seeks to establish the economic and social conditions which contribute to the creation and maintenance of particular types of political systems, while Holt and Turner wish to discover what role political structures should play to maximize economic growth at various stages of economic development. Holt and Turner's study is executed more rigorously—they explicitly state their hypotheses and thoroughly examine the available data in an effort to test them. Although he tends at times to resort to validation by illustration, Moore, too, has written a stimulating study.

While not discussing political development in the way the topic usually is treated, *The Founding of New Societies* (Harcourt, Brace & World, 1964), edited by Louis Hartz, also is relevant. Studies of the United States, Canada, Australia, South Africa, and Latin America provide a basis for arguing that each system's politics has followed the course it has because of contrasts in fundamental values. Because different groups from various European countries settled these areas at different times, they brought with them contrasting fragments of European culture, thereby establishing dissimilar value systems.

The series of studies published by Princeton University Press on political development provides an essential foundation for further examination of this topic. Most of these volumes, edited by various political scientists, contain a number of essays on a wide variety of countries. Unfortunately, the variety is so great that the editors frequently have great difficulty in suggesting any coherent, integrated, and significant generalizations derivable from the essays. A recent volume in the series is Joseph LaPalombara and Myron Weiner, eds., *Political Parties and Political Development* (Princeton University Press, 1966); it lists the titles and editors of the preceding collections. An ambitious one-volume treatment of many of the key issues of political development is David Apter's *The Politics of Modernization* (University of Chicago Press, 1965). His effort to provide an integrated conceptual framework for understanding the most significant aspects of political development is likely to prove difficult reading for those with limited background in this area. While most of the book focuses on "developing" or "modernizing" countries, the final chapter examines the implications of his discussion for democratic government in modern political systems. Another effort, which is proving influential, to state a theory of development is Cyril Black, *The Dynamics of Modernization* (Harper & Row, 1966). Black attempts to distinguish and characterize various stages of development. Finally, because of the important points he makes about institutionalization and participation, Huntington's article cited in note 2 to Chapter 3 should be read.

On revolutions, Brinton's book list in note 7 to Chapter 3 remains a basic starting point despite the drawbacks of being more historical description than penetrating analysis and of employing a rather unconvincing disease analogy. Still it does contain a good deal of useful information on four major revolutions and seeks to compare and contrast their chief characteristics. In *Revolutionary Change* (Little, Brown, 1966) Chalmers Johnson offers a conceptual framework for the study of revolutions with theoretical implications of the factors causing revolutions to develop in particular ways. He also provides a taxonomy for classifying revolutions. Although he gives examples to illustrate his ideas, he does not utilize them for a rigorous study of revolutions. Similarly the monographs mentioned in note 7 to Chapter 3, from the Princeton Center of International Studies group concerned with irregular political change tend to be more conceptual than substantive. Additional results of this group's investigations are collected in *Internal War* (Free Press, 1964), edited by Harry Eckstein.

CHAPTER 4

As note 2 to Chapter 4 indicates, further study of political participation should begin with Milbrath's summary of the most significant research on this topic. Stein Rokkan has been devoting much of his recent research to comparative political behavior. Some of the results appear in two articles in the *International Social Science Bulletin*: "Party Preference and Opinion Patterns in Western Europe," VII:4 (1955), 575–96 and "Introduction to Citizen Participation in Political Life," XII:1 (1960), 7–14. The latter, concentrating on Norway and the United States, also serves to introduce studies by several political scientists of voting behavior in seven countries; only one of these—by Rokkan and Angus Campbell—is not a single-country study. Although focusing on only one aspect of voting behavior, H. Daudt's *Floating Voters and the Floating Vote* (Kroese, 1961) examines for the United States and Britain that segment of the electorate which may play the most crucial role in determining the outcome of elections in many democracies. Alford's study cited in note 6 to Chapter 4 examines the relative impact of class, religion, and region upon party voting preference in Canada, Australia, Britain, and the United States.

Despite its briefness, Douglas Rae's *The Political Consequences of Electoral Laws* (Yale University Press, 1967) is one of the best studies of the impact of electoral systems. A well-conceived research design explicitly stated and thoroughly executed make his findings especially significant. Since Rae's main concern is to marshall empirical evidence, his work can be supplemented with the Leys' article mentioned in note 10 to Chapter 4, which confines itself to the logic of voter party preference under various electoral systems. Although to some extent a form of special pleading for a change in the British electoral system, the Lakeman and Lambert book listed in note 9 is a useful compendium of information concerning the electoral systems employed in a large number of countries. Unfortunately for their main thesis, they at times present only illustrative evidence and fail to provide some of the relevant data.

A good foundation for further study of parties is Neil McDonald's *The Study of Political Parties* (Random House, 1955) and Frederick Engelmann's "A Critique of Recent Writings on Political Parties," *Journal of Politics*, XIX (August 1957), 423–40. While neither of these is concerned primarily to report the empirical findings of party studies, they discuss and evaluate the approaches employed. McDonald attempts to formulate a conceptual framework for the study of parties which is instructive even though the emphasis is heavily upon American parties. Despite its many failures, Duverger's work listed in note 9 repays reading as a pioneering effort to integrate a considerable amount of information about parties into a coherent scheme as an essential first step to making the study of parties analytical rather than simply descriptive. In fact, few political scientists have attempted to improve on Duverger's effort to combine the empirical with the theoretical. In some ways Leon Epstein's *Political Parties in Western Democracies* (Praeger, 1967) is a successor to Duverger in attempting to formulate a theory of party development and function on the basis of evidence drawn from several Western political systems. In *Political Oppositions in Western Democracies* (Yale University Press, 1966) the editor, Robert Dahl, in the concluding chapters seeks to discover, from the individual country studies comprising the bulk of the book, the general characteristics of party competition in democracies and the impact of party competition on political stability. As mentioned in the suggested reading for Chapter 2, Lipset and Rokkan are concerned with the same issue, but discuss it in terms of historical developments in their introductory essay to *Party Systems and Voter Alignments* (Free

Press, 1967). Their volume includes studies of parties and voting behavior by experts on political systems in many parts of the world. The interesting question of how parties finance their operations is examined by several authors in the November 1963 issue of the *Journal of Politics*, volume XXV. Arnold Heidenheimer provides a summary essay on the findings of the individual studies.

As indicated in Chapter 4 there is no satisfactory core volume dealing comparatively with the activity of political groups—the Ehrmann volume mentioned in note 17 is simply a collection of separate national studies. The books available either concentrate on groups in a particular country or on a particular type of group, for example, the military or labor, in several countries. Thus a student can follow up whichever group or country he is most interested in through the titles listed in notes 16 to 21. One important title not mentioned there is J. Roland Pennock's "Responsible Government, Separation of Powers, and Special Interests: Agricultural Subsidies in Britain and America," *American Political Science Review*, LVI (September 1962), 621–33, in which evidence is presented to challenge the belief that the British parliamentary system is better able to withstand group pressures than is the American separation of powers system. Pennock's argument throws significant light on these two systems and thus has a broader comparative relevance.

CHAPTER 5

Given the different approach used in this chapter to the topics discussed, few books are directly relevant. Some of the more traditional or orthodox volumes covering various structures examined in this chapter are cited in note 3 to Chapter 5. In addition to these, *Constitutions and Constitutional Trends Since World War II* (2nd ed., New York University Press, 1955), edited by Arnold Zurcher, discusses the general function of constitutions and the specific content of the constitutions drawn up primarily in Western Europe, but also in East Central Europe, following World War II.

Knowledge of the basic characteristics of the classic presidential and parliamentary systems as elaborated by Douglas Verney in *Analysis of Political Systems* (Free Press, 1959) is a good foundation for further examining executive-legislative relations. While not a summary of research findings, Jean Meynaud's "The Executive in the Modern State," *International Social Science Bulletin*, X:2 (1958), 171–98 provides an introductory orientation to some of the key aspects of this topic. Following Meynaud's article are individual country studies of four Western and two Communist political systems. Similarly Meynaud offers "Introduction: General Study of Parliamentarians," *International Social Science Journal*, XIII:4

(1961), 513–44. Some idea of the difficulties legislatures experience in maintaining control of executive power can be obtained from John Kersell, *Parliamentary Supervision of Delegated Legislation in the United Kingdom, Australia, New Zealand, and Canada* (Stevens, 1960).

As indicated in note 14 to this chapter, Heady's book is the best beginning for comparative studies of bureaucracies. A shorter work of his also seeking to provide a framework for analysis of bureaucracies is "Bureaucratic Theory and Comparative Administration," *Administrative Science Quarterly*, III (March 1959), 509–25. Although not as comprehensive, the Harris and Kearney article cited in note 14 is valuable for discussing the ways in which culture and environment affect administrative systems. On this topic, as for previous ones, I have assumed implicitly that students have followed my previous suggestion of examining the titles in the Princeton political development series. *Bureaucracy and Political Development* (1963), edited by Joseph LaPalombara, is a relevant collection of studies, some raising general questions about the study of bureaucracies, others being comparative investigations, and still others focusing on a single country in an effort to substantiate propositions of general application.

Federalism has been subject to both exceedingly dull, traditional study and stimulating and rigorous examination, especially if it is considered broadly to include not only existing federal systems but also attempts toward integrating well-established national systems as in the European Economic Community. For example, although his conclusions about the impact of federalism on governmental policy have been challenged severely, William Riker has, in the work cited in note 11, broken sharply with the traditional approach and has attempted to specify and test hypotheses concerning the formation and operation of federal systems. Similarly in *Political Unification* (Holt, Rinehart & Winston, 1965), Amitai Etzioni provides a logically well-integrated conceptual framework for the study of federalism, which he applies to several successful and unsuccessful attempts to unify separate political systems, in order to determine the validity of several hypotheses concerning this process. A good discussion of the approaches of four of the most prominent writers on political integration is "Approaches to the Study of Federalism," *Political Studies*, XIV (February 1966), 15–33, by Anthony Birch. Birch evaluates their work in part by examining the extent to which each of these four helps to explain the experience of three British Commonwealth underdeveloped federations. In *Federalism, Finance and Social Legislation in Canada, Australia, and the United States* (Oxford University Press, 1955) Birch investigates comparatively some of the most contentious issues in national-subnational relations.

CHAPTER 6

Further study of elites can begin with Suzanne Keller's *Beyond the Ruling Class* (Random House, 1963) which, after discussing some of the historical and theoretical background of this topic, examines the functions, roles, power, and selection of leaders, concluding with a consideration of the implications for democracy. Although much of the empirical data is drawn from the United States, a number of other political systems are considered as well. This book can be usefully supplemented with the Rustow article (note 3 to Chapter 6) and Lester Seligman, "Elite Recruitment and Political Development," *Journal of Politics*, XXVI (August 1964), 612–26. The latter article, while rather abstract, covers a topic mentioned only very briefly by Keller. After examining these introductory works, *Political Leadership in Industrialized Societies* (Wiley, 1967), edited by Lewis Edinger, should be consulted. The essays included vary from studies of leaders in a single country to theoretical aspects of leadership study to investigation of leader characteristics or roles across national boundaries. An extensive annotated bibliography is a valuable part of the book.

Two interrelated factors which greatly affect the way in which political power is distributed in a society are the educational system and the composition of bureaucracies. John Price discusses these points in "Education and the Civil Service in Europe," *Western Political Quarterly*, X (December 1957), 817–32. Somewhat less comparative, since it is concerned mainly with France and only slightly with Britain, but similar is Frederick Ridley, "French Technocracy and Comparative Government," *Political Studies*, XIV (February 1966), 34–52. Although not always as comparative or empirical as one would prefer, three studies of elites in non-Western systems should be mentioned to augment the areas covered by the previously cited titles. Immanuel Wallerstein, "Elites in French-Speaking West Africa: The Social Basis of Ideas," *Journal of Modern African Studies*, III (May 1965), 1–33; H. J. Benda, "Non-Western Intelligentsia as Political Elites," *Australian Journal of Political History*, VI (November 1960), 205–18; and "Symposium on 'African Elites,'" *International Social Science Bulletin*, VIII (1956), 413–88.

As I indicated in Chapter 6, community power studies making cross-national comparisons are virtually nonexistent. And the United States is by far the leading research site for single-country studies. Polsby (note 4 to this chapter) is the best place to begin further reading on this topic. Two books published more recently that deserve mention are Robert Agger, et al., *The Rulers and the Ruled* (Wiley, 1964), which employs a decision-making approach to the study of four American communities, and Robert Presthus, *Men at the Top* (Oxford University Press, 1964), which attempts to use both the Hunter and the Dahl approaches in examining two American communities.

Although suggestions for further readings on political parties were made in a previous chapter, one book should be mentioned to supplement note 8. Samuel Beer's *British Politics in the Collectivist Age* (Knopf, 1965) is no more comparative than is McKenzie's book. In so far as Beer dissents from McKenzie's views on power relations within British parties, however, further reading on party leadership should include both books. Relevant to assessing party leaders' power is ascertaining the extent to which a party is divided into conflicting groups. Raphael Zariski discusses some of the factors affecting factionalism, drawing illustrative examples from Western Europe in "Party Factions and Comparative Politics," *Midwest Journal of Political Science*, IV (February 1960), 27–51.

CHAPTER 7

I already have cited in note 1 to this chapter the items that those wishing to learn more about structural functionalism should read. To these can be added William Mitchell, *The American Polity* (Free Press, 1962), which attempts to apply this approach to the American political process much more thoroughly than most of its adherents do in their empirical analysis.

The wither-the-discipline issue seems to be discussed almost endlessly. Some of the relevant literature has been mentioned in the suggsted readings for Chapter 1. The problems of comparative political research and some possible remedies are discussed by several prominent political scientists in the first issue of *Comparative Politics*, published in 1968. One of the contributors to this issue (which published papers presented at a conference at New York University earlier in the year) is Roy Macridis, who comments on the extent to which his diagnosis and prescription of 1955 (note 5 to this chapter) was correct.

Index

Abelson, Robert, 197
Aberle, D. F., 195, 204
Abraham, Henry, 201
achievement values, 54
Adu, A. L., 201
Africa, 25, 27, 36, 144
    party systems, 96–98
    political groups, 106–111
Agger, Robert, 215
Albinski, Henry, 208
Alford, Robert, 87, 89, 189, 192,
    199, 205, 212
Almond, Gabriel, 33, 40, 42, 43,
    73, 80, 104, 183–187, 195–
    196, 199, 200, 203, 204,
    205, 208
Ameller, Michel, 201
American Civil Liberties Union,
    18
American Medical Association, 26,
    105
analytical framework, defined, 10
Anderson, Charles W., 200, 201
Andorra, 14
Apter, David, 195, 204, 207, 210
Arendt, Hannah, 198
Argentina, 138
Aristotle, 1, 2
Arizona, 23
Armstrong, John, 202
Article 48 (Weimar Germany),
    119
Article 81 (West Germany), 120,
    121

ascription values, 54
Asia, 27, 28, 36, 37, 144
    political groups, 106–107, 110
Ataturk, 177
Australia, 30, 31, 32, 70, 80, 83,
    137, 138, 192, 210
    class voting in, 87–90
    political parties, 134–135, 141
Australian Labor Party, 88, 134,
    135, 141
Austria, 138
authoritarian personality, 157
authority patterns, 209

Bailey, Stephen, 208
Banks, Arthur, 29, 32, 137, 138,
    200, 209
Basic Law (West Germany), 119,
    120
bathtub gin, 154
Beer, Samuel, 216
Belgium, 93, 94
Benda, H. J., 215
Berg, Elliot, 201
Biafra, 25
Bill of Rights
    Britain, 32
    United States, 30
Birch, A. H., 202, 214
Black, Cyril, 211
Braibanti, Ralph, 203
Brazil, 28, 108
Brezhnev, Leonid, 147
Brinton, Crane, 198, 211

Britain, 15, 16, 23, 32, 33, 43, 45, 55, 57, 60, 80, 84, 92, 104, 119, 135, 142, 150, 161, 192
  bureaucracy, 145–146, 147
  class voting in, 87–90
  interest groups, 103–104
  national/local relations, 139–141
  party cohesion, 128–129, 130–133
  reform of Parliament, 124–126
  role of Parliament, 9–10
British Commonwealth, 80, 214
Brown, Bernard, 208
Bryce, James, 187
bureaucracy, bureaucrats, 50–51, 52, 54, 63, 100, 107–108, 162
  nonprofessionalized, 142, 143–144, 147–149
  popular attitudes toward, 33, 42, 144–145, 147, 150
  professionalized, 142–143, 144–147, 150
bureaucratic elite system, 149
Butler, David E., 205
Butler, Jeffrey, 201

California, 23
Campbell, Angus, 199, 211
Canada, 30, 32, 70, 80, 93, 138, 141, 150, 192, 210
  class voting in, 87–90
  political parties, 132–134, 135, 136
  recruitment of legislators, 154–156
Cantril, Hadley, 34, 42, 196
Cassinelli, C. W., 200
centralized political system, 51–54, 57, 60, 63, 66, 67, 73, 139, 140–141
Ceylon, 44, 148, 160, 161
Chapman, Brian, 201
charisma, 35, 37, 38, 73
Charlesworth, James, 204, 208
China, 12, 56, 159

Christian Democrats
  Italy, 89, 136
  West Germany, 119, 121
Civic Culture, The, 43, 104, 105, 186, 187, 188, 193
Civil War (United States), 90
class voting, 87–90, 132, 189
Cole, Taylor, 201, 205
Coleman, James, 27, 97, 184, 195, 196, 197, 200, 201, 203, 208
Colonial Office (Britain), 23
communes, 78
Communists, 34, 96, 136, 161, 165
  China, 159, 161
  U.S.S.R., 59, 99–100, 146, 159
community power studies, 162–164, 166
comparative analysis, utility of, 4–6, 7–8, 155
"Comparative Political Systems" (Almond), 183
conceptualization, 188–189, 193
Congo, 25, 45
Connecticut, 3
Connery, Robert, 208
Conservative Party (Britain), 13
constitutional guarantees, 31–32, 119, 174–175
constitutional tinkering, 117, 118–128, 129, 149, 151
constitutions, functions of, 31–32
constructive vote of no confidence, 120
Converse, Philip, 199
Council of Ministers (Fifth Republic France), 123
coup, 74–75, 77–78, 110, 175
  defined, 75
cross-national studies, value of, 4–8
Cross-Polity Survey, A, 29, 32, 44, 45, 97, 137
cross pressures, 197
  theory of, 40–41
Cutright, Phillips, 28, 29, 195, 208
Czechoslovakia, 28, 48

Dahl, Robert, 190, 191, 203, 205, 212, 216
Daudt, Hans, 211
Davies, James, 198
decentalized political systems, 51, 54, 60, 61, 66, 67, 140–141, 149, 175
decision-making approach, 163–164
Declaration of the Rights of Man (France), 32
de Gaulle, Charles, 73, 123, 124, 125
demands
    expression of, 11–14, 83–114, 118
    processing of, 14–15, 118
democracy(ies), 48, 49, 51, 59–61, 63, 71, 73, 80, 83, 89, 90, 99, 106, 107, 121, 159, 168, 171–172, 174–177, 186–188, 197
    characteristics of, 29, 168
    requisites for, 21–23, 26–46
Democratic Party (United States), 86, 90
Denmark, 94
de Schweintz, Karl, Jr., 196, 197
Deutsch, Karl, 209
dictatorship, 27, 28, 56, 63, 67, 79, 102, 198
dissolution power, 129–132
Dominican Republic, 44
Double Helix, The, 191
Dupeux, George, 199
Duverger, Maurice, 92, 164, 189, 200, 204, 205, 212

East Germany, 28
Easton, David, 195
Eckstein, Harry, 200, 204, 209, 211
ecological correlation, 87, 199
economic development, 48–49, 88–89, 98, 107, 144, 147, 184

level of, and democracy, 26–29, 45–46, 67–68, 82, 176
level of, and self-government, 23–24
process of, 46, 50–74, 77, 81, 89–90, 176, 197, 198
Edinger, Lewis, 215
education, 72, 84, 85, 88, 89, 111, 112, 114, 158, 159–160
    impact on political culture, 42–44
    as a means of control, 62–63
Ehrmann, Henry, 200
Eisenhower, Dwight, 127, 174
elections, 13, 170–171
electoral system, 91–96, 113, 121, 131, 150–151, 189
elite rule, 162–177
emergency powers, 119
Enclosure Act (Britain), 55
Englemann, Frederick, 212
English Constitution, The, 3
Epstein, Leon, 202, 212
Escape From Freedom, 176
Ethiopia, 148
Etzioni, Amitai, 214
Europe, 27, 28, 56, 89, 144
European Economic Community, 25, 214
executive instability, 5, 120–121, 129, 145
executive power, 121–124, 149

Farrell, Robert, 208
Fascists, 159, 161
Federal Bureau of Investigation, 48
federalism, 88, 137–142, 149
Finer, S. E., 201
Flanagan, William, 204
Flaten, Arnold, 173
Fogelman, Edwin, 204
Foreign Affairs Committee (United States), 124
Foreign Relations Committee (United States), 124

Form, William, 203
France, 5, 12–13, 34, 55, 56, 73,
    86, 96, 97, 124, 130, 133,
    140, 141, 155, 161, 171
  bureaucracy, 107, 144–146, 147
  Fifth Republic, 16, 22, 73,
    123
  Fourth Republic, 16, 92, 109,
    122, 123, 129, 131, 133,
    145, 192
  Third Republic, 122, 123, 129,
    145
Franco, 22
free enterprise, relation to democ-
    racy, 29–30
French Revolution, 73
Fromm, Erich, 176
functional approach, 11

Galbraith, John K., 174
Germany (cf. also East Germany
    and West Germany), 26
  modernization by nationalistic
    regime, 56–59
  Nazi regime, 56–59, 81–82, 99,
    100, 121
  Weimar Republic, 17, 22, 27,
    81–82, 92, 94, 119, 120,
    121, 122
Gibralter, 22
government ownership of business,
    29–31, 89
Grand Coalition (West Ger-
    many), 119
Greece, 28
Gregg, Phillip, 209
Gregor, James, 186, 204
group membership
  cumulative, 41
  overlapping, 41–42
Grumm, John, 200
guild system, 56

Hamburger, Ernest, 196
Harris, Richard, 203, 214
Hartz, Louis, 210

Heady, Ferrel, 202, 214
Heer, Friedrich, 197
Hegel, Georg Wilhelm Friedrich,
    47
Heidenheimer, Arnold, 213
Hermens, Ferdinand, 189, 204
Herz, John, 198
historicism, 47–48
Hitler, Adolf, 13, 27, 82, 119
Hobbes, Thomas, 2
Hoffman, Stanley, 209
Holt, Robert, 197, 204, 210
House of Commons (British), 7,
    83, 92, 125, 128
Hunter, Floyd, 203, 216
Huntington, Samuel, 72, 81, 96,
    197, 198, 211

India, 23, 44, 138, 148, 160
industrialization, 52–74, 107, 176
institutional approach, 9–10, 115–
    117, 118, 127, 131–132,
    183
institutionalized political struc-
    tures, 71–72, 73, 81, 96,
    113, 177, 198
  defined, 71
interest groups, 13, 40, 43, 45,
    65, 100–101, 102–104, 175,
    185, 200–201
  associational, 38, 46, 68, 71,
    105–106, 107, 110, 112,
    113, 188
  informal, 104–105
  institutional, 36, 38, 71, 106,
    107–112, 114, 118
    defined, 106
  nonassociational, 71, 106, 107,
    113
    defined, 36, 106
intermediate groups, 70, 71
Italy, 26, 27, 33, 34, 41, 43, 80,
    84, 89, 92, 104, 105, 128,
    131, 136
  modernization by nationalistic
    regime, 56–59

Janos, Andrew, 198
Janowitz, Morris, 201
Japan, 144, 160
Johnson, Chalmers, 198, 211
Johnson, John, 201
Johnson, Lyndon B., 124, 127
Jones, Charles O., 202
judicial review, 128

Kahin, George, 196
Kearney, Robert, 203, 214
Keller, Suzanne, 215
Kendall, Willmoore, 199
Kersell, John, 214
Kilson, Martin, 200
Kling, Merle, 198
Kornberg, Allan, 202, 203
Kornhauser, William, 197, 199
Kosygin, Alexei, 147
Kulaks, 59
Kuomintang Central Executive
    Committee, 161
Kuroda, Yasumasa, 203

Labour Party (Britain), 13, 129,
    133, 135, 145
Lakeman, Enid, 200, 212
Lambert, James, 200, 212
LaPalombara, Joseph, 197, 200,
    210, 214
Lasswell, Harold, 203
Latin America, 27, 28, 36, 75, 106,
    107, 108, 154, 210
  military in politics, 110–112
leaders
  characteristics of, 157–162
  control of, 167–170
  motivation of, 157–159
  recruitment of, 154–157, 161
legitimacy, 70, 77, 79–82, 101–
    102, 109, 177
Leites, Nathan, 133, 202
Lenin, 165
Lerner, Daniel, 195, 203
Levy, Marion, Jr., 204
Leys, Colin, 200

Liberal Party (Britain), 92, 135
Liberal Party (Canada), 141
Lipset, Seymour Martin, 27, 43,
    44, 79, 80, 195, 196, 197,
    198, 199, 208, 212
Lipson, Leslie, 200
Livingston, William, 202
Luce, Clare Boothe, 159

Macrae, Duncan, Jr., 192, 205
Macridis, Roy, 188, 204, 205, 207,
    208, 216
Malaysia, 35, 138, 148
Maldive Islands, 23
mandate doctrine, 13
Marx, Karl, 47, 165
McDonald, Neil, 212
McKenzie, Robert, 135, 202, 204,
    216
McWhinney, Edward, 202
Mechan, J. Lloyd, 196
mercantilism, 51
Merritt, Richard, 209
Merton, Robert, 204
Mexico, 33, 34, 43, 80, 84, 104,
    122, 138
Meynaud, Jean, 213
Milbrath, Lester, 199, 203, 211
military forces, 50, 77, 114, 149,
    150, 154, 175
  role in politics, 36, 108–112
Miller, Delbert, 203
Millin, Bruce, 200
Mills, C. Wright, 174, 203
Mitchell, William, 216
modern political systems, 34–35,
    37–40, 45, 46, 48, 49, 81,
    176
Monroe, James, 37
Moore, Barrington, Jr., 197, 210
Morgenthau, Hans, 124
multilateral force (MLF), 21
Mussolini, Benito, 13

National Association for the Ad-
    vancement of Colored Peo-
    ple, 106

National Association of Manufacturers, 106
national identity, sense of, 88
nationalism, 26, 73
Nazis (National Socialist German Workers' Party), 21, 43, 81, 82, 92, 99, 100, 119, 121, 159, 161, 170
Near East, 106, 107, 109, 110
Needler, Martin, 201
Nenni Socialists, 89
Netherlands, 94
Neubauer, Deane, 196, 208
New Zealand, 30, 31, 32, 80, 83, 87, 92
Nigeria, 22, 25, 138
Nkrumah, Kwame, 177
Noltes, Ernst, 209
Nordlinger, Eric, 209
North Atlantic Treaty Organization, 21
North, Barbara, 200, 205
North, Robert, 200, 205
Northern Ireland, 139, 140
Norway, 85, 86
NPD (Nationaldemokratische Partei Deutschlands), 151
Nyerere, Julius, 177

Organski, A. F. K., 197

Pakistan, 122, 138, 148, 149
Paris Commune of 1870, 73
parliamentary system, 120, 122–123, 124–126, 128– 137
Parsons, Talcott, 204
party identification, 85–86, 96
Party and Society, 189
party systems, 91, 92, 121, 148, 150, 189
  competitive, 28, 29, 98, 102, 161, 177
  multiparty, 5, 86, 92–96, 113, 114, 136, 141, 145, 184
  noncompetitive, 96–99, 102
  two-party, 92–95, 113, 141

Party Systems and Voter Alignments, 190
peasant revolution, 56, 58
peasants' garden plots (U.S.S.R.), 30, 66
Pennock, J. Roland, 213
Pentagon, 106
Pettit, Lawrence, 208
Philippines, 44
Pitts, Jesse, 209
Plato, 173
pluralism, 40–42, 164, 174
political culture, 32–34, 68, 121, 133, 147, 175, 186–188, 193, 210
  concept of, defined, 16
  in modern systems, 37
    coercive, 37–38, 39
    consensual, 39–40, 45, 72
    fragmented, 38–39, 72, 74
  relation to political stability, 16–18
  in transitional systems, 35–37
political development, 28–29
  in contemporary developing nations, 68–74
  during early industrialization, 53–61, 64–65
  during later industrialization, 61–64, 65–68
  measures of, 48–49
  during nation-building stage, 50–53, 69
Political Oppositions in Western Democracies, 190
political participation, 42, 71–73, 80–81, 83, 84–85, 110–111, 114, 170–171, 172, 177, 180, 187
  partisan, 85–87
political parties, 13, 36, 38, 70, 72–73, 88, 93, 94, 95, 118, 148, 156
  cohesion of, 103, 125–127, 128–137, 145, 150, 192
  mass, 132

political parties (*contd.*)
  participation in, 85–87
  power structure, 135–136, 141–142, 164, 169–170
  role of, 99–102, 112–114, 121, 169, 175, 184–185
political process, 118
  analytical stages of, 11–15
political science, aims, 4–5, 8, 19, 208
politicize, defined, 17
politics
  defined, 2
  importance of, 1–4, 18–19
Politics of Developing Areas, The, 184
Polsby, Nelson, 203, 215
Pool, Ithiel de Sola, 197
Porter, John, 203
Powell, G. Bingham, Jr., 183
prefects, 140
Presthus, Robert, 216
Price, John, 215
primitive societies, 2
Prince of Wales, 3
Pure Food and Drug Act, 30
Pye, Lucian, 196

Quebec, 90
Queen Victoria, 3

Rae, Douglas, 189, 205, 212
Ranney, Austin, 199, 202, 208
Rasmussen, Jorgen, 202
Rayburn, Sam, 127
regent government, 14–15, 164–165, 174, 180
regional political cleavages, 88, 90
religion, 161
  impact on party preference, 87, 88, 90
replicative studies, 6–7, 192
  defined, 6
Republican Party (United States), 86

revolution, 74–82, 176–177, 181
  defined, 74–75
  conditions productive of, 75–77, 198
Revolutionary War (American), 37
Ridley, Frederick, 215
Riker, William, 137, 138, 202, 214
Rokkan, Stein, 190, 199, 208, 209, 211, 212
role, 116, 117, 124, 133–136, 140, 149, 150
  concept of, defined, 11
Roosevelt, Franklin D., 165
Rosberg, Carl, 97, 200, 201
Rule, James, 198
rules of the game, 133, 134, 136
Runciman, William, 199
Russett, Bruce, 209
Russia, 47, 56, 59
Rustow, Dankwart, 203, 215

safe seats, 130, 131
San Marino, 14
Sartori, Giovanni, 200
Scandinavia, 3, 90, 92, 94, 184, 185
self-confident citizen, 39, 40, 42, 45, 80, 172, 174, 175–176
  characterized, 32–34
self-government
  impact of world wars on, 23
  requisites for, 23–26
Seligman, Lester, 215
Senegal, 110
separation of powers system, 122–127, 128, 132, 133
Shannon, Lyle, 195
Sierra Leone, 4
Singapore, 35
Smith, Margaret Chase, 159
Social Democrats (Germany), 89, 119
social mobility, 53, 54, 64, 111
Social Science Research Council's Committee on Research in Comparative Politics, 192

Socialist Party (Norway), 86
Somit, Albert, 195, 207
South Asia, 159
soviets, 78
Soviet Union, 12, 14, 15, 18, 28,
    30, 31, 43, 48, 98, 99–100,
    106, 108, 138, 174
  bureaucracy, 146–147
  economic development in, 65–67
Spain, 22
Spanish American War, 22
specialist legislative committees,
    103, 124–125, 126
Spiro, Herbert J., 201
spurious relation, defined, 5
stability of political systems, 15–
    17, 70, 71–74, 81, 90, 92,
    172, 181–182, 198, 209
Stalin, 18, 31
Stamps, Norman, 209
Stewart, J. D., 200
Stokes, Donald, 205
structural analysis, 11, 116–118,
    132–133, 135, 149,–150,
    193
structural functionalism, 179–181,
    188
  utility of, 182–183, 186, 193
  weakness of, 181–182, 183–186
structures, 116, 188
  concept of, defined, 11
  primary, 37
  secondary, 37
Sudan, 110
Survey Research Center, Univer-
    sity of Michigan, 192
Sutton, F. X., 204
Sweden, 30, 161
Switzerland, 28, 30, 94, 137, 138
system, concept of, defined, 11

Tanenhaus, Joseph, 195, 207
taxonomy, 34–35
  defined, 34
team research, 189–192
Tennessee Valley Authority, 30

Textor, Robert, 29, 137, 138, 200,
    209
Thailand, 107, 149
Thomas, Norman, 203
Tilly, Charles, 198
totalitarian political system, 38, 46,
    73, 78–79, 98, 99, 100–101,
    113, 176
traditional societies, 68, 81, 148,
    176, 196
transitional political system, 34–37,
    38, 40, 81, 113, 114, 184,
    196
Turkey, 108, 109, 161
Turner, John, 197, 210

Unger, Aryeh, 200
unitary system, 137, 139, 140, 141,
    149
United Nations General Assembly,
    23
United States, 11, 14, 15, 16, 21,
    22, 23, 27, 29, 30, 31, 33,
    37, 41, 43, 45, 48, 49, 70,
    76, 80, 83, 84, 92, 96, 108,
    119, 130, 131, 137, 160,
    161, 163, 165, 169, 170,
    175, 210
  bureaucracy, 145–146, 147
  class voting in, 87–91
  Congress, 11, 49, 106, 128, 134,
    138, 139, 150, 192
    recruitment of members, 154–
      156
    relations with President, 122–
      123, 124–127
    role of, 9–10
  economic development, 59–60,
    61–62, 64
  interest groups, 102–106
  national/local relations, 138–
    141
  partisan political participation,
    85–87
  party cohesion, 128, 132–133,
    134–135

urbanization, 56, 62–63, 70, 77, 89, 107, 114

Valen, Henry, 199
Venezuela, 138
Verba, Sidney, 33, 40–43, 73, 80, 105, 186–187, 196, 197, 199, 200, 204, 208
Verney, Douglas, 213
Viereck, Peter, 209
Vietnam, 22, 124, 169
von der Mehden, Fred, 201, 203

Wallerstein, Immanuel, 215
Washington, George, 37, 123
Watson, James, 191, 205
Weiner, Myron, 197–198, 200, 210
West Germany, 21, 33, 43, 80, 84, 95, 104, 105, 138, 139, 141, 161, 162

West Germany (*contd.*)
    bureaucracy, 144–146, 147
    constitutional tinkering in, 119–121, 150–151
Wheare, K. C., 137, 138, 139, 201
Wildavsky, Aaron, 200, 202
Williams, John, 205
Wiseman, H. V., 204
Wolf, Charles, Jr., 196, 197
World War I, 22, 27, 58
World War II, 27

Young, Michael, 204
Young, Oran, 183, 204
Young, Roland, 208
Yugoslavia, 138

Zariski, Raphael, 216
Zurcher, Arnold, 213